A Miracle Named Jesus

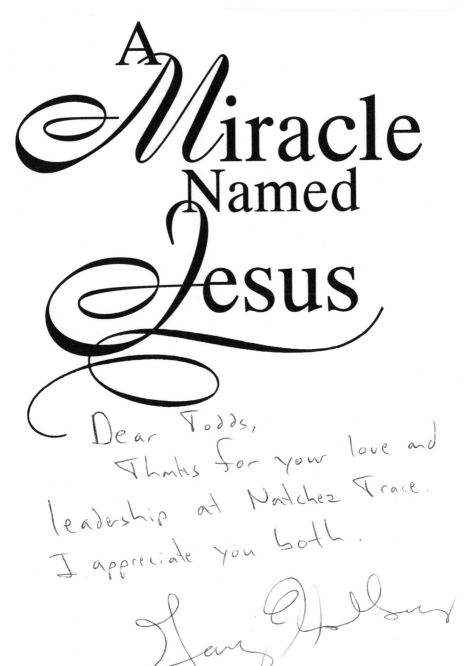

Dear Todds,
Thanks for your love and
leadership at Natchez Trace.
I appreciate you both.

Gary Holloway

 COLLEGE PRESS
PUBLISHING COMPANY
Joplin, Missouri

Library of Congress Cataloging-in-Publication Data

Holloway, Gary, 1956–
    A miracle named Jesus/Gary Holloway.
      p.   cm.
    ISBN 0-89900-780-5 (pbk.)
    1. Jesus Christ—Miracles. I. Title.
  BT366.H65 1997
  232.9'55—dc21   97-1838
                                    CIP

To the memory of Henry A. McDaniel, Jr.,

who shared the miracle of Jesus

with all around him.

CONTENTS

INTRODUCTION

"It's a miracle!"

We hear it frequently, particularly on the lips of emotional and charismatic Christians. For them, miracles, from finding the lost car keys to healing inoperable cancer, happen daily.

"It's a miracle."

For others of us who are Christians, such a statement doesn't sit well. Yes, we believe God answers prayer. Yes, we believe he works in our world. But what many call miracles — finding a parking spot at the supermarket, getting a phone call from a friend you're thinking of, finding the lost airline tickets — seem beneath the dignity of the Almighty. To some, the word "miracle" smacks of charlatan faith-healers, greedy TV preachers, and manipulators of the spiritually ignorant. So we hesitate to use "miracle" for God's current actions, reserving it to describe his works in the biblical past.

I believe that certain gifts of the Holy Spirit were intended only for the early church. God gave signs such as healing, tongue-speaking, and other miraculous gifts to confirm his word to the apostles. Soon after the death of the last apostle, these gifts and signs ended.

But miracles still happen. God is still a God of power, a God of healing, a God of miracles. I don't believe he gives individuals, faith healers, the power to heal. I do believe he hears our prayers for healing and miracles. He not only can heal today, he does.

Why do I believe it? Because it's biblical. The Bible teaches us to pray for daily bread, for healing, for faith, for courage, for anything and everything we need from God. We are told to pray in faith and not doubt. Faith in what? Faith that God will hear and will do something. If God acts, what can we call that but a miracle? Indeed we might even define a miracle as *an event that would not have happened had we not prayed to God and God had not acted.*

Some of us may still be nervous about this talk of miracles. Why? Perhaps because we have a warped view of natural law. We think belief in miracles means we must abandon the idea of an orderly universe of cause and effect. But natural law simply refers to the regularity we see in nature. Regularity, however, does not mean uniformity. If God enters an event as cause, we still have cause and effect. In other words, we should look for regularity not in nature itself, but in the God who made nature.

In place of "miracle," some Christians are more comfortable with the term "providence" to refer to God's work in our world today. "Providence" is a particularly slippery term. One can argue it is a biblical concept, but not a biblical word. "Providence" became a popular way to describe God's activity in the age of rationalism and deism. That age believed providence to be God's "ordinary" work in creation and was not to be confused with miracle. They said God now works only through natural law.

From that view it is only a short step to practically denying God's healing and wonder-working power. Many in our churches avoid both "miracle" and "providence." We hardly speak of God's present action, assuming he completed his work in Bible times. We pray as an obligation, not because we think God will actually "do" something. Or if we do expect him to act, we expect he will in normal scientific and technical ways: "Guide the hands of the physicians," we pray.

If God guides the hands of the physicians, isn't that more than "natural"? Isn't it a miracle? Doesn't God heal today? Of course he does! He heals through medicine and physicians. He also heals without them. As a non-charismatic, I don't believe he gives individuals the power to heal as he gave power to Jesus, Peter, and Paul, but I know he hears our prayers and works his will. It's a miracle!

To begin to understand the miraculous power of God in our world today, we must return to the world of the Bible, to the world of the early disciples who saw the power of God at work in a man. A man named Jesus. A "man accredited by God to you by miracles, wonders, and signs, which God did among you through him . . ." (Acts 2:22). A man, but more than a man, the Son of God.

Some Christians are charismatic. Some are not. But all agree on Jesus. By looking at the miracles of Jesus, we can see them as "wonders and signs." They are more than just startling, unusual events. They point as signs to the God who loves us. In the miracles of Jesus, we who believe focus on the Divine Presence who is active everywhere. We come to see the presence of him who loves us and saves us, not just in these strange events, but in every event of life.

So, I invite you into this strange world of the miracles of Jesus. A world where the blind are healed, the lame walk, the demon-possessed are freed, where we drink miraculous wine, walk on water, and even rise from the dead. By entering this world we come to see that it is our world. That the power that worked through Jesus still works in our lives through faith. That God still heals the sick, comforts the grieving, defeats the devil, and rules the winds and waves.

CHAPTER ONE

A NICE LITTLE MIRACLE

John 2:1-11

". . . but you have saved the best till now" John 2:10.

I missed my sister-in-law's wedding.

I was at the church, on time, but I missed the ceremony. I was preparing the reception.

For those who know me well, this revelation is a shock, for I am no cook, caterer, or expert on wedding etiquette. I helped with the reception for one reason alone: there was no one else to do it.

You see, Gwen (my sister-in-law) and Rush (her husband to be) are very laid back people. They thought it would be nice, instead of a formal reception, to have a simple bring-finger-foods picnic-type of affair after the wedding. They'd asked a few people to bring sandwiches and snacks, but they had forgotten a few things. Like plates, napkins, drinks, and (most importantly) to put anyone in charge.

So while Gwen and Rush exchanged vows, I found myself setting up tables, running to the store, setting out food, scrambling to get it all done before the wedding guests came in.

It went off without a hitch. Gwen and Rush and their guests had no idea there had been any problem.

What would have happened if I hadn't stepped in? Someone else would have, I'm sure. Or at worst, the food would not have been served and there would have been a mild embarrassment. This wedding experience reminds me of another wedding long ago.

The Wedding

It was a small wedding in a small town in a small corner of the world. The bride and groom were like countless others who had gone before. The ceremony was traditional with no surprises. The problem came with the wedding feast.

As was the custom, the feast was an elaborate affair, lasting for days and involving everyone in the village. Preparations had been underway for weeks, women stood over boiling cookpots, men set up tables in the town square, even the children were busy gathering wildflowers for decorations. Finally all was ready.

The bride and groom and the wedding guests arrived. All had plenty to eat and drink. This pleased the man in charge, the master of the feast.

Then disaster struck. A servant went to a wine jar and found it empty. No problem. He'd just find another. But it was empty too, as was the next, and the next. What was he to do? Run to the master of the feast and say, "We've run out of wine"? The master would be furious. No wedding was complete without wine. The guests would soon complain. The bride and groom would face embarrassment. The one perfect day of their lives would be forever ruined.

The servant did not know what to do. He had no money to buy wine. Even if he did, the closest village was miles away and he couldn't get there and back before the feast ended. What could he do? Nothing but tell the master of the feast the truth. There was no more wine.

However, a kind woman was there, a guest from Nazareth. He mentioned the problem to her, and she mentioned it to her son. At first he seemed reluctant to help. "Why do you involve me?" he asked his mother. But the woman told the servant, "Do whatever my son tells you."

All fine and good, but what could her son, Jesus, do? Where could he find wine for all these people? "You see those six jars over there?" Jesus told the servant, "Fill them with water."

The jars in question were huge, each holding twenty to thirty gallons. So the servant called his fellow workers and they filled the jars. It made no sense, but what could they lose?

"Draw out some water and take it to the master of the banquet," Jesus said.

"This will never work," thought the servant. "Does this Jesus really think the master can't tell water from wine?" But in his desperation, he did what Jesus commanded.

"Here you are, master, more wine for you to taste." As the master tasted the water, the servant cowered, expecting a blow for trying to fool him so obviously. But he finished the cup and smiled. "This is the best wine I've ever tasted," he said, complimenting the groom for his generosity. As the servant took the cup, he looked inside. It was wine! He couldn't believe it! He took a sip himself. It was true! By one small act this Jesus had turned the wedding from a disaster to a complete success.

The First Miracle

John tells us this was the first "sign" or miracle that Jesus performed. It's not what we might expect as the first miracle. After all, wouldn't we expect Jesus to begin his ministry with a bang? We want a dramatic and public miracle, maybe healing someone blind from birth or walking on water or even raising someone from the dead. We expect a miracle that everyone knows about and no one can deny, so that everyone will come to believe in Jesus.

Instead Jesus gives us a nice little miracle. A miracle, to be sure, to take ordinary water and turn it into the best wine, 120 to 150 gallons of it! Still, it was a miracle that few saw. The guests are unaware that anything strange had happened. The master of the feast marvels only at the quality of the wine. Who even knew a miracle had taken place? Mary, the servants, Jesus, and his disciples. How do we know the disciples knew? John tells us, "This, the first of his miraculous signs, Jesus performed at Cana in Galilee. He thus revealed his glory, and his disciples put their faith in him" (John 2:11).

So why begin a ministry with such a quiet miracle? Perhaps because, as Jesus told Mary, his time had not yet come. The day would come when Jesus would heal the blind and raise the dead, when all would confront the question of his identity, when the choice to follow him or crucify him would be clear. For now, Jesus was content to raise a small band of followers, the disciples. This small sign was for them, so they would put their faith in him.

Signs by their very nature point to things beyond themselves. So too, this sign of Jesus points to God the Father. What can we learn about our heavenly Father from a wedding feast long ago?

A God of Little Things

Our God is an awesome God. He is the Lord of Hosts, the Creator of the Universe, and the King of Kings. The far-flung planets, the wind and waves, the burning flames of the angels, he commands them all with a single word.

Can such a God care for us? We can imagine him dealing with presidents and kings, with the wealthy and powerful, with the rich and famous. But can he care for ordinary people, like you and me? Can we even imagine that the Almighty King of the Universe can take the time to deal with the problems of people like us, nobodies that the world doesn't notice?

"I'm not a nobody," you may say, "I'm a very important person." Are you? Who knows you beyond your circle of family, friends, and business acquaintances? Do you own a business? Good and well, but won't it continue when you're gone? Do your children love you? Wonderful, but will your great-grandchildren even remember your name? At times, we may be impressed by our importance, but in our saner moments we know that we are ordinary people, "just plain folks," who will never be on television, never meet the President, never have a candy bar named after us.

Can the Almighty care for us? Indeed, he does. He cared enough to send his Son for us. He sent him not in trappings of fame and glory, but to an ordinary girl, in an ordinary town. Born not in a palace, but in a stable. Wrapped not in royal robes, but in humble strips of cloth. Not on a throne, but in a manger. In the face of Christ, we see a God who cares for ordinary people.

We see it in his first miracle. Jesus does not go to Rome or even to Jerusalem. He comes to Cana, a backwater village. He doesn't perform this wonder at the temple on a feast day, but in the village square at an ordinary wedding. He helps not a king, but an ordinary couple. He turns water into wine to save little people in a little town from a little embarrassment. He does it as a sign. A sign that points to the God who cares about the most insignificant moment in the most ordinary day of our humdrum lives.

This is good news beyond our imagination. For if you are like me, you are just an ordinary person. Each day is much like the one before and the one to come. We raise our families, work at our jobs, and live from paycheck to paycheck. We go to church and worship God each Sunday much as we worshiped him the week before. We find ourselves praying the same old prayers, sinning the same old sins, dreaming the same old dreams.

Suddenly we find our lives interrupted. Illness strikes. Death claims a loved one. A child marries. We become grandparents. In the peaks and valleys of our lives, it is easy to see the hand of God. He brought this great blessing. He comforts in this great sorrow.

It is harder to see his hand on an ordinary afternoon of an ordinary Tuesday. But he is there and he cares. His Son cared enough to go to an ordinary wedding at an ordinary town and do an extraordinary thing. To insure the joy of the most important day of their lives, he turned water into wine. This same Jesus has the power to turn our hours and days, whether ordinary or important, into times where his power and glory are seen. Even three o'clock on Tuesday can be a sign that points to the God who cares, the God for whom there are no little towns, little things, or little people.

A God of Celebration

Religious people have a reputation for being a joyless lot. Today, when you tell people you're a Christian, they sometimes react with, "Well, I'll have to watch my language," or "Then I guess there'll be no fun around here." Since some forms of worldly "fun" are sinful, those around us assume Christians condemn all enjoyment. Christians are always serious, always judgmental, always spoiling the fun.

It was the same in Jesus' day. The religious people, the scribes and the Pharisees, were certainly serious folk. They clearly condemned the ungodliness of their time. They kept the commandments faithfully. They fasted often. To them, the joys of the world were snares to avoid. They followed God, not pleasure.

Which is why they opposed Jesus. He didn't take his religion seriously enough! He didn't fast like the Pharisees and John the Baptist. He was always breaking the rules the Pharisees had made to protect the Law. He even enjoyed weddings and parties with unacceptable people. He even turned water into wine! No wonder his contemporaries called him "a glutton and a drunkard, a friend of tax collectors and 'sinners'" (Matthew 11:19).

It's easy to misunderstand Jesus. Some did in his own time and accused him of hedonism. But when he said, "Life's a party," he did not intend a shallow, empty numbing of the pain of life, what people call partying today. Instead he called for a return to God, the source of true joy and happiness, the One who made wine and food and sex for humans to enjoy, not to abuse. He is our Father who desires true joy for all his children.

Jesus turned water into wine. Not a little water and a little wine, but a prodigious amount: 120 to 180 gallons of it. Jesus knew how to celebrate the God of abundance. He came to give not just an abundance of wine, but an abundance of life: "I have come that they may have life, and have it abundantly" (John 10:10, NRSV). In this small act in a small town we catch a glimpse of the God who "is able to accomplish abundantly far more than we can ask or imagine" (Ephesians 3:20, NRSV). Jesus teaches us how to enjoy the abundance of God.

In light of the abuse of alcohol in our society, abstinence may be the best policy for Christians. But we are disloyal to Jesus if we let our abstinence from alcohol sour our entire outlook on life in this world. Christians alone are the true party animals, inviting others to the greatest party of all: the eternal kingdom of God where there is always laughter and no tears. We do the world a disservice if we let them think Christians are boring or prudes or party-poopers.

Jesus liked parties. He even brought the wine.

The God of Transformation

"There is nothing new under the sun," says the writer of Ecclesiastes. In a world that changes daily, with new technology, new information, and new products without number, it is strange to say that there is nothing new. Yet the older one gets, the more it seems that one has seen it all before. Life becomes flat, stale, and predictable. Today looks a lot like yesterday, and tomorrow will be more of the same. We long for some new thrill, for new energy, for a new outlook on life.

But life disappoints us. All the new things we try to revitalize our lives soon become old and emptied of their meaning. If only somehow our humdrum existence could be transformed into something new!

Jesus took the most ordinary thing in the world, plain old water, and transformed it into the extraordinary, the best wine. I don't think it is reading too much into the story to see more here than a simple chemical change. What Jesus did at Cana, he can do in each of us. He takes our ordinary, plain, humdrum lives and transforms them into something new, something special. With Jesus in us, even the ordinary tasks of life become meaningful, for we do them in his name and to his glory.

So this sign reminds us of the God we serve. He and he alone can make things new in our lives. God promises a truly new deal: forgiveness of sin, a law in our hearts, and knowledge of the Lord himself. All come from God's initiative and action, not from our human efforts to do something new. God will do "new things, . . . hidden things unknown to you," (Isaiah 48:6). He will give us a new name (Isaiah 62:2), changing things so radically that it will be like making a new heaven and a new earth (Isaiah 66:22). God promises a new start, a fresh beginning.

That promise becomes true in Jesus. He comes as something old, the Messiah, the one the Jews had expected for centuries. But something is new about his coming, so new that those who looked for the Messiah couldn't see him when he came. When God sends something new, it truly is new — so new we fail to recognize it. So new we may even fight against it.

So Jesus' contemporaries didn't understand the new thing God was doing among them. They criticized Jesus for not following the old paths: "Why do your disciples eat and drink, when the disciples of John and those of the Pharisees fast and pray?" In answer, Jesus unveiled the new:

> He told them this parable: "No one tears a patch from a new garment and sews it on an old one. If he does, he will have torn the new garment, and the patch from the new will not match the old. And no one pours new wine into old wineskins. If he does, the new wine will burst the skins, the wine will run out and the wineskins will be ruined. No, new wine must be poured into new wineskins" Luke 5:36-38.

The old wineskins of progress, change, and improvement cannot contain the newness of the gospel. This new strong wine is from God's own vineyard. It's not the results of our efforts. Human thought, plan, and technique won't contain it. Human packaging or marketing can't improve it. It can only be enjoyed for what it is: the free and gracious gift of God.

The Pharisees couldn't understand it. It was completely new to their experience. Modern Americans hooked on change and novelty can't understand it either, for it is the last thing we expect: something really new. Even Christians caught in the rut of the boring sameness of constant change may forget the kept promise of God: "If anyone is in Christ, he is a new creation; the old has gone, the new new has come!" (2 Corinthians 5:17).

The Son of Glory

Turning water into wine is a sign of God's care for little people. It is a sign of God's abundant blessings for all. It is a sign of God's transforming power. Most importantly, it is a sign of Jesus' character. At the end of the story of turning water to wine, John tells us: "This, the first of his miraculous signs, Jesus performed in Cana of Galilee. He thus revealed his glory, and his disciples put their faith in him" (John 2:11).

The disciples already believed in Jesus. Andrew had already told his brother Simon, "We have found the Messiah" (John 1:41). But now, having witnessed the sign at Cana, they come to a new level of faith: they see the glory of Jesus.

"Glory" in our day usually means praise and honor for a great deed. We speak of those who have won glory on the battlefield. In the Bible, the word has a slightly different flavor: it refers to the overpowering, holy presence of God himself. In the Old Testament, when the tabernacle was completed, the cloud covered it and the glory of the Lord filled it (Exodus 40:34). Throughout the Old Testament, the phrase "the glory of the Lord" refers to God's special presence with his people.

When the disciples saw Jesus turn the water into wine, they saw a sign that pointed them to a greater truth: this Jesus shares in the very nature of God, he has God's glory. Like God the Father, he cares for those the world ignores. Like God, he gives abundantly. Like God, he has the power to change the ordinary into the extraordinary.

As we look at his miracle two millennia later, may we also see more than just a nice little miracle. May we see in this small act the Jesus who cares, who gives, who changes us. That change, like the miracle, takes place in obedience. "Do whatever he tells you," Mary told the servants. And they did. By his power and through their obedience the water becomes wine. In the same way, it is not our power but his that changes us, yet this power comes through a long obedience. May we each day see signs of his glory in our lives and respond by doing whatever he wills.

Then we too will truly be his disciples.

CHAPTER TWO

I SEE

John 9:1-41

"One thing I do know. I was blind but now I see!" John 9:25.

Imagine.

Imagine a typical spring day.

You get up early in the morning to see the sun rise. Soon you can make out the shadowy outlines of houses and trees. Suddenly, the sun peeps above the horizon and the world begins to take shape and color. The grass and trees are a riot of shades of green. Flowers of all colors and shapes are in bloom. A squirrel scampers through a tree. Birds sing. A new day begins.

Imagine.

You turn from the window to see the sleepy but still impish face of your son. He grins and asks, "What's for breakfast?" He's soon joined by the most beautiful sight in the world: your daughter's shining smile. A new day has truly begun.

A Great Miracle

Imagine.

Imagine that you've never seen a sunrise or a sunset, a flower, a tree, a squirrel, a bird. What's more, you've never seen the face of your father or mother or husband or wife or children. Imagine being born blind.

One man doesn't have to imagine. He is blind, blind

from birth. In his day vocational training for the blind consisted of giving them a bowl and telling them to beg. So he sits in the same spot day after day, begging enough to barely stay alive. After a while, he's not the only one who is blind, for the hundreds who pass him day after day, even those who throw a few coins in his bowl, soon pass by without looking at him, with unseeing eyes as if he were part of the landscape.

Until the day a young Rabbi came along.

His disciples saw the blind man and asked the Rabbi, "Who sinned, this man or his parents, that he was born blind?" The disciples cannot see the man. They cannot see him as a fellow human being, but only as the occasion for a theological discussion. Perhaps they were showing off for their Master, trying to prove what profound thoughts they had. But the man was blind, not deaf! What must he have thought to be used as an example of a terrible sinner, so terrible that God cursed him with blindness? But the disciples were blind to his feelings.

The Rabbi is different. He sees the man, not a test case for a theological argument, but as one who suffers. He sees an occasion for healing. "Neither this man nor his parents sinned," said Jesus, "but this happened so that the work of God might be displayed in his life." Calling himself "the light of the world," Rabbi Jesus proceeds to bring light to the life of the blind man.

He doesn't heal him with a word or with a touch, like he had done to countless others. Instead he spits on the ground, makes mud, and puts it on the man's eyes. He says, "Go wash in the pool of Siloam." Why this strange method of healing? I don't know. Perhaps he did it this way to test the man's faith. Perhaps he did it this way because this is how men were healed in Old Testament times. Perhaps the ways of this Rabbi Jesus will always be strange to us. But he puts mud on his eyes and tells him, "Go wash."

The man goes to the pool and washes his eyes and for the first time in his life, he sees. He must have jumped for joy! "So that's what they mean by 'sky'. And that's a tree and a bird and a flower. Why didn't someone tell me the world was so beautiful? Are they all blind? And this, this the most amazing sight of all: my mother's face." In the midst of his joy and celebration, he lost sight of Jesus, the one who healed him.

A Greater Miracle

This was indeed a great miracle, one unheard of. Indeed, the blind man, now seeing, will himself later exclaim, "Nobody has ever heard of opening the eyes of a man born blind" (John 9:32). Even today, if we were to hear of one blinded in an accident who now can see, we might try to explain it away as a psychosomatic cure: there was no physical problem, only a psychological block to sight. But blindness from birth must be physical, not psychological. Its cure is truly a miracle.

A greater miracle is here, or perhaps we should say a greater wonder. For it is truly a wonder, truly unbelievable, that some could witness this miracle, could know that the blind man they had seen for years by the side of the road now had his vision. That they could hear from the man's own lips that it was Jesus who healed him, and still call Jesus a sinner and refuse to believe in him.

Here is a greater blindness than one who is blind from birth. The Pharisees and the man's own parents shut their eyes to what Jesus had done. They blind themselves to who he is.

What makes them so blind? First, they are *blinded by legalism*. This healing took place on the Sabbath. Such healing is "work" according to the Pharisees, and it is against God's law to work on the Sabbath. Jesus thus is a lawbreaker and sinner and could not have healed this man. However, the only law Jesus had broken was one the religious leaders had made up. It was never against God's law to show compassion. But that made no difference to the Pharisees. Don't confuse them with the facts! Never mind the fact that Jesus had given the man his sight. If the Pharisees said it never happened, it never happened.

The blindness of the Pharisees amazes us. How could they deny their own eyes? But are we any better? Do we ever let our laws, our rules, our understanding of what the Bible says or what God can and cannot do get in the way of what we see with our own eyes? Have we ever denied the power of Jesus in the lives of others because they fail to conform to our notions of what it means to be a Christian? I know Christians who look at the work of Mother Teresa among the lepers of Calcutta, and say it's the work of Satan, just because she is Catholic. We don't have to go that far to see the way legalism blinds. We only have to look in our own church. Or in a mirror.

Legalism isn't the only thing that can blind us to the work of Jesus. The blind man's parents were *blinded by fear.* The Pharisees called the parents in and asked them, "Is this your son? Is this the one you say was born blind? How is it that now he can see?"

"'We know he is our son,' the parents answered, 'and we know he was born blind. But how he can see now, or who opened his eyes, we don't know. Ask him. He is of age; he will speak for himself'" (John 9:20-21).

The parents knew Jesus had healed their son, but they intentionally blinded themselves to the fact. Why? Because they were afraid the Jewish authorities would put them out of the synagogue.

Have you ever let fear blind you to the work of Jesus? At the office when someone else is being ridiculed for acting like a Christian, do you speak up to defend them? Do you say, "I too am a believer?" Or does the fear of being put outside the circle of your friends cause you to keep silent or say, "Let him speak for himself. It's none of my business."

Have you ever let fear keep you from doing the work of Jesus? Why do we not evangelize? Because we're afraid of being rejected or being thought closed-minded or fanatical? Why don't we help families we know are in trouble? Because we're afraid to get involved? Why don't we help the stranger at the side of the road who begs from us as this blind man did? Fear of strangers? Fear of foolishly throwing our money away? Fear that he might want more than money? He might want a friend.

We are not to be foolish in our faith, but we are to be courageous. Not a day goes by in our culture that we are not frightened into silence like these parents. May God give us courage to confess what we see: that through his Son the lame walk, the deaf hear, the blind see.

Ultimately the Pharisees are *blinded by willful igno-rance.* Jesus tells them, "If you were blind, you would not be guilty of sin; but now that you claim you can see, your guilt remains" (John 9:41). Unlike the blind man, their blindness is not from birth. They intentionally made themselves blind to Jesus. They saw the good he did and called it evil. Refusing to believe their own eyes, they are blinder than the blind man ever was, for they blind them-selves to the only one who can cure them.

Are We Blind?

Do we blind ourselves to Jesus? Do we fail at times to see his power at work? I fear we do. We sometimes fail to see him at work in the church. The church where I preach is a small one, about seventy people. As a small church we don't have the multitudes of programs and ministries that mark larger churches. Because of that, I sometimes hear, "We've got to get this church going. We've got to get organized. We've got to do something besides just sitting in the pews." Sometimes I hear these statements from my own mouth.

No doubt we can do more, but I wonder if these statements reveal our blindness to what Jesus is already doing in our midst. When I look out from the pulpit on Sunday morning, I see people whose faith and dedication I can never hope to match. There sit the Burtons who parent four adopted children and who spend their spare time building houses for the homeless. There's Rugel, a physician who for years has worked part-time in medical missions in Guatemala. In the back sit the Duttons, the real shepherds of our church who have been second parents to every child in the congregation (including me). On the front row are the Farmers, Therold who does the song leading and Lucretia who teaches Bible school.

The list goes on and on. Don Kelley cares for our building and takes calls from those needing financial help. When Don is gone, we don't know what to do. There's Camille who works with the Women's Shelter. Joyce who talks to her friends about Jesus. Chuck who studies the Bible deeply and shares his knowledge with us. Here are parents who give themselves to raising Christlike children. Here are courageous teenagers who maintain their faith in hostile situations. Here are Myrtie and Hazel, widows who encourage us by their very presence. And there are dozens more I have failed to name.

I know these people. I know their faith and good works. I know them well enough to know that their courage and faithfulness do not come naturally. They are the result of a miracle. They come from the hand of the One who put mud on a blind man's eyes.

These people are in your church too, living lives of quiet faith and service. We must not be blind to what Jesus is doing in our churches. Ministries and programs and ministry teams are fine and good, but we must not limit the power of Jesus to them. He works in every church through those that love him.

We may be blind to his work in the church, but also to his work in the world. If we read the morning paper or watch the evening news, it seems the world is completely in the clutches of the evil one. Children starve. The innocent are slaughtered in war. The rich get richer. The poor cannot afford justice. Corruption pervades our political system. Has God abandoned his world?

No. It is still our Father's world. But we see his hand and the healing hand of his Son only through faith. It may appear that evil has the upper hand, but we believe that God is at work in our world, sometimes boldly, sometimes silently. He has not abandoned us, but sent his own Son to redeem the world. We believe that the day will come when what we see, and what the world is blind to, will be seen by all. Every knee will bow, every tongue will confess, every eye will see the healing hand of Jesus.

The Greatest Miracle

We may be blind to the power of Jesus in our world and our church. What is worse, we may be blind to his power in our own lives. To be blind from birth is a problem, to say the least. But the blind man had another need more severe than his need for sight.

After Jesus healed him, the blind man lost sight of Jesus. The Pharisees command him to denounce Jesus as a sinner. He replied, "Whether he is a sinner or not, I don't know. One thing I do know. I was blind but now I see!" (John 9:25).

The blind man had never seen Jesus. He wasn't sure who Jesus was. But he did know what Jesus had done for him, and he refused to blind himself to the power of Jesus. The Pharisees responded by insulting him, calling him a disciple of Jesus. Finally they gave him the punishment his parents feared: they threw him out of the synagogue.

So Jesus found him again. Having given him the gift of sight, Jesus now gives him an even greater gift, the gift of faith.

Jesus heard that they had thrown him out, and when he found him, he said, "Do you believe in the Son of Man?"

"Who is he, sir?" the man asked. "Tell me so that I may believe in him."

Jesus said, "You have now seen him; in fact, he is the one speaking with you."

Then the man said, "Lord I believe," and he worshiped him (John 9:35-38).

It was truly a day of miracles and wonders. A wonder that a man born blind should see. A greater wonder that some could see the healing and still be blind to Jesus. But the greatest wonder is that the Son of Man came to save sinners by calling them to faith. The blind man was overjoyed to see grass and trees and flowers and his mother's face. But the greatest thing he saw that day was the face of the one who healed him, the one who came to save.

I pray we will never know what it's like to be blind. We can't really imagine what it must have been like to see for the first time. It's also hard to believe that there are still people in our world who refuse to see Jesus for who he is, who can see the powerful works of creation and redemption and fail to see the hand behind them.

Or is it hard? True, we have not been born blind. But what is worse, we have blinded ourselves to the work of Jesus. We have turned our backs on him through sin. The greatest miracle is not that Jesus healed the man born blind, but that he sought us out when we were blind to his love. He put his hands on us and healed. He told us to wash, not in the pool of Siloam, but in the waters of baptism. He heals our sins not by mud, but by his own blood. By his hand, and by that washing, and by his blood he gave us new sight, new life.

The blind man goes and washes, but he does not heal himself. On his own he is still blind. His sight comes as a gift. So also with us. We come to Jesus as unworthy sinners. He heals us not because we deserve it, but because he has compassion. No words say it better than the words of the old hymn by Charlotte Elliott:

Just as I am!
poor, wretched, blind–
Sight, riches, healing of the mind,
Yea, all I need in Thee to find,–
O Lamb of God, I come! I come!

We come. He heals.

Before this miracle, Jesus tells the disciples, "I am the light of the world" (John 9:5). "Light" is one of John's favorite words for Jesus. He contrasts it with the darkness of sin. What separates Christians from the blindness of the world is not our innate niceness or our good works. We are different because we see the Light. We believe in him.

As those who walk in the light, we can see what others cannot. By faith we see the hand of Jesus in our churches, our world, and our lives. We see that the poor may be rich in faith, those who suffer can rejoice in God, and the meek will truly inherit the earth. We should not be surprised when those around us think us strange visionaries and accuse us of refusing to face reality. In Christ, we see realities they cannot see. Our eyes are opened.

That doesn't mean we have all the answers. No one fully understands Jesus. Even we who have served him all the years of our lives must confess that we see him only dimly. But no matter how weak our faith, like the blind man we know one thing for certain.

We were blind.

Now we see.

So we worship him.

CHAPTER THREE

TWO WOMEN, ONE STORY

Luke 8:43-48; 13:10-13

". . . but no one could heal her" Luke 8:43.

In central Texas we have a malady called cedar fever. An allergy that hits hardest in January, it can make life nearly unbearable with runny nose, congestion, aches, and (as its name implies) even fever.

Last week it hit me so hard I did two things I rarely do: I went to the doctor, and I stayed home from work. At home I tried to read and breathe and rest, but the antihistamines the doctor gave me made me pace around my living room, looking out the window at a beautiful warm Texas January day, but afraid to go outside and face the pollen. It was so strange to be at home in the middle of the day. No one was on the streets. I could hear few sounds from outside my window. The sense of isolation was so intense that I could easily believe I was the last person on the face of the earth.

As I stood there at the window feeling miserable and somewhat sorry for myself, I suddenly thought of Maurice and immediately felt ashamed of my whining. Maurice is a dear friend, a minister with unbounded energy who taught me what it means to care for people. A few years ago he contracted a strange disease that the doctors had trouble identifying, much less curing. The disease is chronic, progressive, and painful. As a result, this active man has been forced to quit the ministry and be confined to his home.

To me, this is the worst kind of sickness. To be stricken suddenly with heart disease or a fast-moving cancer is certainly a tragedy, but this is as bad as it gets. Maurice stays home every day, isolated from others by pain and slow debilitation. He faces a mystery, going from doctor to doctor receiving differing treatments, all (at best) only partially effective.

In my battle with the little nagging illness of cedar fever, I've tried all kind of cures — vitamins, nose sprays, antihistamines — that give only partial relief. What must it be like to be Maurice? Yet he faces his illness with courage and faith, accepting what the hand of the Lord has given him without losing his hope.

Nobody

There was a woman whose nagging chronic illness exiled her from those around her. She had a hemorrhage that would not stop. The loss of blood made her weak, unable to do all the things her neighbors took for granted, but that wasn't the only reason for her isolation. She was a Jew, and (according to the Old Testament) as a woman with a discharge of blood, she was "unclean" (Leviticus 15:25-27).

Unclean. The word itself is enough to make one ashamed to be around other people. "She's unclean," they would whisper when they thought she couldn't hear. But she did hear and was ashamed.

It's not only the word that isolated her. The Old Testament law was explicit on what it meant to be unclean. No one was to touch her. Any bed she slept on, any chair she sat in was unclean. If anyone even touched them, they too would be ceremonially unclean and would have to bathe to rid themselves of her curse. What is more, in her day Jewish tradition excluded the unclean from the synagogue. She was never allowed to sing or pray or be comforted by the Scriptures in the company of her neighbors.

Think of her pain, physical and spiritual. How often she must have looked out her window and wished, "If only I could be like them; if only I could be normal for a day, even an hour." Worse than anything was her guilt, for she felt somehow it must be her own fault that she was unclean. Over and over again the question sounded in her head, "Why? Why me? What have I done to deserve this?" No answer came. She suffered like this for days, weeks, and years. Twelve years.

Still, she had hope. She heard of a physician who could help her, so she went to try his cure. It did no good. Then she heard of another who'd had success with her kind of problem. His treatments were painful and expensive. They didn't help. She went to physician after physician, desperate for a cure, until her money ran out.

She found herself still in pain, still weak, still isolated from her neighbors, still having to worship alone. Now, to make things worse, she was in poverty, having spent all she owned on physicians. She spent her days alone in her house, a refugee from society An exile. A nobody. Unclean.

Somebody

Until the day she heard of Jesus. We don't know how she heard about him. Perhaps one of the few friends she had left told her of his marvelous power. Perhaps in one of her infrequent trips to the village square she had overheard talk that this miracle worker was coming to her town.

But how was she to see him? He was not a doctor with office hours. Wherever he went, a crowd pressed against him. She was unclean. She must keep away from crowds. What if she tried to see him and someone recognized her? "Get out of here!" they'd say. "What are you trying to do, make the Master unclean?" If that were to happen, she knew she would die of embarrassment.

But she was desperate. This was her last and only chance to be healed, to be clean, to be a human being again. She'd heard so many stories of the power of this Jesus that she knew he could heal with just a touch. Did he even have to know he had healed her? Couldn't she remain anonymous, just touch him in a crowd, and still be healed?

"It's worth a try," she thought. So she wrapped her veil around her face, left her home, and found the crowd surrounding Jesus. Pushing her way through it, she saw him for the first time. Like all Jewish men, he wore tassels on the end of his robe. Reaching down when no one was looking, she touched one of them.

Suddenly she felt an energy she hadn't felt in years. Her bleeding stopped! The long nightmare of pain and isolation was over! She had rejoined the human race. "Now," she thought, "all I have to do is to slip away unnoticed."

But it was not to be.

"Someone touched me," Jesus said. "I know that power has gone out of me."

In those few words, Jesus said so much. *"Someone touched me."* This woman who had been an exile, a refugee, a nobody, was now a somebody. By touching Jesus, he changed her status forever. She is no longer just a sick, nameless woman. To Jesus, she is somebody.

"Someone *touched* me," Jesus said. "You see the people crowding against you," his disciples answered, "and yet you can ask, 'Who touched me?'" (Mark 5:31). The disciples find the question humorous. "Of course someone touched you," they think. But there are different kinds of touches. The jostle of the crowd is not at all the same as the woman's touch. She touched him with her need. Jesus always feels the touch of those in pain.

"I know that power has gone out of me." Power. That is what the woman needed. Power to be healed. Power to be clean. Power to be whole. Power to face the world again. Jesus gives her that power. And it costs him something! The power went out of him, it drained him. Jesus never gives without cost to himself. His greatest gift cost his life.

"Somebody touched me," he said. With those few words he destroys the woman's plans. Now she cannot hide. Now she cannot keep silent. She has been found out. All will know that an unclean woman had the audacity to touch the holy Master. But she must own up to what she has done. She must confess. Jesus has left her no choice.

So she comes, trembling with fright and embarrassment. She who for years has lived on the margins of society is now the center of attention. Falling at the feet of Jesus, she tells her story: the bleeding, the pain, the weakness, the isolation, the years of searching, the touch, the power, the healing. What will the Master say to her? Will he rebuke her for her presumption? Chide her for her cowardice? Scold her for her shyness?

He does none of these. He praises her. "Daughter, your faith has healed you. Go in peace" (Luke 8:47). We might look at this poor woman and see a coward, one whose faith is so weak she will not confront Jesus directly with her request, but instead goes literally behind his back. Where we see cowardice and desperation, Jesus sees faith. For twelve years this woman has tried all kinds of cures, all false hopes. But when Jesus comes she has the faith to touch him. And that is faith enough.

"Go in peace," he tells her. The Hebrew word for peace, *shalom*, is more than just "good-bye." *Shalom* or peace is the word for wholeness, for being in harmony with the world, your neighbor, and your God. Jesus gives the woman more than physical relief; he makes her whole. He restores her to fellowship with the human race. Now she is clean. Now she can visit her neighbors, shop in the market-place, and attend the synagogue. Now her heart is at peace.

Everybody

Her story is our story. How do we come to Jesus? We come with sickness. For many of us, that sickness is minor. For others, their illness is chronic and incurable, much like this woman's. Where do we go when we are sick? We go to doctors, as she did. We should, for many times they can help us. Do we take our illness to Jesus? Perhaps that depends on how bad we feel. I guarantee I took my cedar fever to him as well as to the doctor. And he healed me! No doubt the shot and the medicine the doctor pre-scribed helped too, but even when we go to the doctor, it is Jesus that heals. Let us not be embarrassed to bring our physical illnesses to him, no matter how trivial or serious. He cares about our health. He cares about us.

Like this woman we also come to Jesus unclean. Oh, we don't believe we are ceremonially unclean as in the Old Testament, but which of us at times has not felt "unclean?" Perhaps sickness makes us feel that way. Our nagging pains and weakness frustrate us because we can-not do what we once did, we cannot be our best. We're irritable, hard to get along with, and it is no wonder that others avoid us. Or at least we think they do. Like this woman, we feel cut off from those around us. No one understands. We are alone.

There are other reasons we feel unclean, reasons that are not our fault. Rape victims feel that way. They are not to blame, but they still feel as if everyone is looking at them. Everyone knows. Everyone condemns. Divorced people feel that way. Even when they have done all they can to keep the marriage together, divorce makes them feel like failures, isolated from their married friends. Even those who are widowed may feel unclean. Now they don't fit in. They're a fifth wheel. Those who used to invite them and their spouses to dinner, now neglect to invite them. They somehow have become invisible. Unclean.

Depression makes one unclean. Each day is a struggle to just get out of bed. One doesn't want to do anything or see anybody. We need someone to talk to, but that's the last thing we want to do. No one understands. We withdraw from those around us, but we believe they withdrew from us. We feel unclean.

Sin makes us unclean. Perhaps none of the situations above result from sin. Maybe they do. Even if we are not sick, or victims, or divorced, or widowed, we feel unclean. We feel guilty. We feel guilty because we are guilty. People may look at us and see exemplary Christians, people who have it all together. We know better. We know our hearts have turned from God. We know we've turned them from compassion to our neighbor. "Sin" may not be a fashionable word in our society. It may smack of low self-esteem, of puritanical repression, of an unenlightened past. But in our heart of hearts we know there is no better word to describe ourselves. We are sinners. Unclean.

So we come to Jesus. Sick. Unclean. Weak. Too weak to help ourselves. We come desperate, having tried all the physicians of body and soul, finding no relief.

Like this woman we may try to come to him secretly. We want his healing but we fear to face him publicly. So we hang around the fringes of the crowd that surrounds him. Perhaps we go to church late and leave early, sitting in the back so no one will notice. We read our Bibles, but we read them alone and tell no one. Finally, out of desperation and faith, we touch him. He heals us.

But he will not leave us alone. He calls us to publicly confess what we have done. Like this woman we tell our story. We were sick, unclean, alone. We touched. He healed. We tell our story not just once but with every moment of every day of our lives. And no matter how shy we are, no matter how weak our faith, with the touch of

39

Jesus it is a faith that makes us whole. To us he also says, "Your faith has saved you; go in peace." To us, as to her, he gives a wholeness, restoring us to God and our neighbors.

All this if we only have the faith to touch.

Another Woman

Like this woman we must overcome all obstacles to get to Jesus: our hopelessness, our fear, the crowd, whatever it may be that gets in our way. We seek, ask, knock, and we keep on without losing heart. Her story is the story of the effort all must make to come to the one who alone can heal.

But there was another woman. She was much like the first. She had an illness that was chronic. Her back was bent, she could not straighten up. No doubt this malady kept her from doing all she wanted. It isolated her from all around her. People avoided her as something misshapen, a cripple, a freak. Though not technically unclean, she must have felt that way.

And she'd been like this longer than the other woman. Eighteen years! There is no mention of her consulting physicians like the first woman. For her condition no one had a cure. She doesn't expect one.

So she goes to the synagogue as she did every Sabbath, expecting nothing unusual. But the unusual happens. Jesus is there. She does not ask him to heal her. She does not sneak behind him and touch the tassels of his robe. Perhaps she doesn't even pay much attention to this young rabbi from Nazareth.

All that does not matter. What matters is: he sees her. Calling her forward, he says, "'Woman, you are set free from your infirmity.' Then he put his hands on her, and immediately she straightened up and praised God" (Luke 13:12-13).

Yes, we seek Jesus. We seek him with all our heart. We push through the crowd to touch him. But let us never forget that he sought us first. He sees. He calls. He touches. He heals.

Two women. One story. Everyone's story. Our story. Most of all, Jesus' story.

When Jesus begins his story, his ministry, he goes to his hometown, stands in the synagogue, opens the scroll of the Scriptures and reads:

> The Spirit of the Lord is on me,
>> because he has anointed me
>> to preach good news to the poor.
> He has sent me to proclaim freedom for the prisoners
>> and recovery of sight for the blind,
> to release the oppressed,
>> to proclaim the year of the Lord's favor (Luke 4:18-19).

The first woman's story: how we come to Jesus. Sick. Weak. Unclean. Trembling. Poor. Captive. Blind. Oppressed. Still we come, to touch and be healed. In the words of the beautiful poem, "Our Master," by John Greenleaf Whittier:

> *The healing of his seamless dress*
> *Is by our beds of pain;*
> *We touch him in life's throng and press,*
> *And we are whole again.*

The second woman's story: it is always Jesus who comes to us. He sees us. He knows our sickness, our pain, our poverty, our oppression. He calls us forward. He touches us. He heals. This is who he is. This is what the Spirit of the Lord anoints him to do.

Two women. One story. No matter what our sickness of body, heart, and soul, he touches, we touch. We feel his power. Trembling we bow before him and tell our story. We tell his story. We praise God. We go in peace.

Now a somebody.

Now whole.

CHAPTER FOUR

THE OTHER GOOD SAMARITAN

Luke 17:11-19

"Were not all ten cleansed? Where are the other nine?" Luke 17:17.

We all know the story of the Good Samaritan (Luke 10:25-37). For some of us, it's our favorite Bible story. It's so familiar that our culture has "Good Samaritan laws" laws to protect from lawsuits those who stop to help others in need.

Let me remind you of the story.

A certain man went down from Jerusalem to Jericho. Robbers beat him, took all he had, and left him to die. A priest came by, saw him, and passed him by. A Levite did the same. But a Samaritan saw him and had pity on him. Dressing his wounds, he took him to an inn and gave the innkeeper money to care for him. When he left, he said, "If he costs you more, let me know. I'll pay for it."

This familiar story shocked those who first heard it. They were shocked by the depth of the man's compassion, but more shocked by his identity. He was a Samaritan, not a Jew. To Jews, he followed a false religion. He and his whole land were to be avoided by strict Jews. But it is this Samaritan, not the priest or the Levite, who proves neighbor to the man.

When was the last time you were a good Samaritan?

Last Friday I looked up from my desk to see a stranger in my doorway. I work in downtown Austin and not a day goes by without my seeing homeless people on the street. Here was one in my office.

"May I help you?" I said (inwardly thinking, "How in the world did you get in here?").

He sat down and told me some of his life story. I listened with one ear, wondering how I could kindly get rid of him. Suddenly I noticed a hospital armband on his wrist, a band from the local mental hospital. My desire to get him out of my office suddenly became more urgent.

"So if you could help me with five dollars, I'd really appreciate it," he said.

I gave him five dollars, told him I had to leave and pick someone up at the airport (which was true), and gently ushered him out the door.

He thanked me.

Was I a Good Samaritan? I'm not sure. I may have done him more harm than good. He may have spent that money on alcohol, not food. I don't get points for pure motives. But I still felt good afterward.

When was the last time you helped a stranger? How did it make you feel? Did he thank you?

The Good Samaritan: The Day After

Now (as Paul Harvey would say) let me tell you the rest of the story. A few days later, as I'm getting out of my car at work, I see the same homeless man. He has slept outside under an awning near our building.

"Can you spare five dollars?" he asks.

I look in my wallet and find it empty. "I'm sorry. I don't have anything for you today."

Coming close, he curses me loudly, calling me every name in the book. I back away slowly, fearing for my safety. Heart pounding, I gain the safety of my office and try to get some work done.

I leave work that evening to find my tires slashed. I call the police and a wrecker and get home late.

The next day, I arrive at the office to find it vandalized. Our computers are smashed, papers are everywhere, books are torn and ruined. The police come again. Later that day they catch the homeless man who admits he did the damage. "They wouldn't help me, so I showed them," he said.

You can imagine how I felt. Violated. Hurt. Disappointed. Angry. I'd tried to help the man and he repaid my help with ingratitude. Is there anything more infuriating than people hurting you for helping them? Isn't ingratitude the greatest sin?

Now for the truth: it never happened. Oh, the first part did, there was such a man and I gave him a few dollars, but he never turned on me. It never happened, but it could have. How many times have we helped people and they have repaid us by ignoring us or (what is worse) by doing us wrong?

Imagine if you will what could have happened a few days after the Good Samaritan left the man at the inn. The man comes to and asks the innkeeper, "How did I get here?" The innkeeper tells him the story of the Good Samaritan. "Give me his address," the wounded man says. So he does.

A few weeks later the Good Samaritan gets a letter in the mail. It's from the wounded man's lawyer. He is suing him for practicing medicine without a license, claiming he would have been better off if the Samaritan had left him alone. He even implies the Samaritan might have had something to do with the robbery.

Farfetched? Or does it have the ring of truth? Isn't this why we have "Good Samaritan Laws" to protect those who help strangers from the threat of lawsuits? Why do we fail to help strangers in need? Fear? Fear that they will turn on us? Or is it because we've helped strangers before and failed to even get a "thank-you" in return? We don't mind doing good if only we'd get a little recognition for it.

The Ten

Jesus had to deal with strangers too. One day Jesus met ten strangers. Lepers. They had a painful disease that disfigured them, cut them off from human contact, and eventually proved fatal. The Jewish historian Josephus said lepers were treated as if they were already dead.

But these "dead" men can talk. They cry out to Jesus from a distance, "Jesus, Master, have pity on us!" (Luke 17:13).

They stand at a distance. They cry out from afar. They are not the first to do so. The Psalmist cries:

> My God, my God, why have you forsaken me?
> > Why are you so far from saving me,
> > so far from the words of my groaning?
> O my God, I cry out by day, but you do not answer,
> > by night, and am not silent (Psalm 22:1-2).

Like the Psalmist who cries to God, the lepers cry out to Jesus from a distance, begging for mercy. They are not the first to do so. They also are not the last. Jesus himself uses the Psalmist's words to cry out from the cross. He knows what these lepers feel. He knows what it is like to feel distant from the Father.

These lepers must have felt abandoned by God. How could this have happened to them? But they are also distant from other humans. Literally they must keep their distance, crying "Unclean, Unclean." Again, with the Psalmist they can cry

> My friends and my companions avoid me
> > because of my wounds;
> my neighbors stay far away (Psalm 38:11).

They cry out from a distance. Far away from man and God. Which of us has not at times felt the same? We feel abandoned by God and by neighbor. We seem so far away from those around us. No one understands. No one really touches us.

We may even resist the one who wants to touch us and heal us. We come to Jesus, but we keep our distance, afraid to get too close because he might want more from us than we are willing to give. He might want it all.

So these lepers stand at a distance, but they have the faith to bridge that gap with loud cries. They do not despair. They still have hope. Jesus, the Master, can save. So they cry out for mercy.

And they are heard!

"Go show yourselves to the priests," Jesus commands.

"Go," Jesus says. As he told the blind man, "Go, wash," so he tells the lepers, "Go, show." Why all this going? By washing or showing were they to earn their salvation from sickness? No. Jesus gives freely. He can heal with a word, a look, a touch. So why does he say "Go"?

It is a test. A test of their faith. Do they believe in the power of Jesus enough to keep his word? They do. And as they go, the incredible happens: they are cleansed. Their leprosy disappears. They are whole.

The Nine and the One

One of the ten who shouted for healing continues to shout. His cry is now one of praise. Leaping, shouting, praising God, he turns back and runs to Jesus. Throwing himself at his feet, he gives thanks.

Then comes the punch line. Luke tells us, ". . . and he was a Samaritan" (Luke 17:16). A Samaritan! False teachers! Pagans! Unclean! Yet he and he alone returns to give thanks.

"Where are the other nine?" Jesus asks. That's what we'd like to know. How in the world could anyone show such ingratitude? They had been healed of an incurable disease, brought back from the dead as it were, and they just go on their way, not taking the time to turn and give thanks. And they are Jews! God's chosen people. They should have known better.

Why didn't the nine return? Were they so caught up in the joy of the miracle that they just forgot? Were they too busy? Were they afraid this Jesus might demand some payment for the miracle if they returned? Afraid he might say, "Follow me?"

We're not told why. It remains a mystery. Beside this, all examples of ingratitude pale. We just can't imagine.

Or can we? How often do we fail to turn and praise and thank? Is this not the whole of the Christian life: that at each moment of each day we live lives that say "thank-you" to the One who saved us? This story of the nine and the one strikes at the very heart of Christian faith.

Just a few verses before the leper story, the disciples cry to Jesus, "Increase our faith!" (Luke 17:5). The episode of the lepers demonstrates two kinds of faith. The nine certainly have faith. They have the faith to cry to Jesus. They believe he can heal them and so they lift their voices. They have faith to trust his command. He says, "Go." They go, believing something will happen.

The nine have faith. Faith to cry out for mercy. Faith to obey the Master's command. Faith to be healed from their dread disease. Such faith seems formidable. Would we have as much?

Yet their faith is woefully inadequate. It lacks one thing necessary for saving faith. True faith is thankful.

True faith focuses on what we have received, not on the good we do for God or for others. Yes, we should do good. Why? Not to receive thanks, not to feel good about ourselves, not to earn our salvation, but because the good we do for God and others is our way of saying "thanks" for the unspeakable gift God has given us: the gift of his Son.

"But that's what we do," you say. "We are not like the nine. We know what Jesus has done for us, and we work hard each day to thank him. All we ask is a little recognition for the good we do."

Many of us are confused about good deeds. Some think we must do more and more so we might prove worthy of salvation. Some think grace means we don't have to bother with good works. Like the nine, we can go on our way and just enjoy what Jesus has done for us. Some of us think we deserve more praise and thanks for the work we do. What would our families, our communities, our businesses, and our churches do without us? They'd fall apart. No one knows the half of all we do. All we want is a word of praise. That would make us happy.

We can learn the wrong lesson from the story of the grateful leper. We might think the lesson is that others should show thanks to us. They should praise us for the good we do. But only One is truly worthy of praise. All our hard work is an inadequate response to the bounty of his gift. Just before the episode of the lepers, Jesus reminds the disciples that they can never earn the praise of God:

"Suppose one of you had a servant plowing or looking after the sheep. Would he say to the servant when he comes in from the field, 'Come along now and sit down to eat'? Would he not rather say, 'Prepare my supper, get yourself ready and wait on me while I eat and drink; after that you may eat and drink'? Would he thank the servant because he did what he was told to do? So you also, when you have done everything you were told to do, should say, 'We are unworthy servants; we have only done our duty'" (Luke 17:7-10).

We can never earn his praise, for we are only doing our duty. We work because he is the Master, we are the slaves. We work to say "thank-you" for the gift we can never repay. We can deserve no thanks in return.

We can never earn his praise, but by his grace he gives it, saying:

"Well done, good and faithful servant! You have been faithful with a few things; I will put you in charge of many things. Come and share your Master's happiness!" (Matthew 25:21).

The secret of the one leper is that he knew the faith that leads to thankfulness. He comes, he bows, he thanks. That same faith leads us to thank God with all we do for him and others, expecting no thanks in return. Yet if we give him ourselves in gratitude, unworthy servants though we be, he graciously calls us to share his happiness. This is the faith that saves.

Two Samaritans

We learn from both Samaritans. From one we learn how to give. We are to help the stranger just because he needs help. All in need are our neighbors. We help, not expecting repayment or even thanks. We help even if those we help turn against us.

From the other good Samaritan we learn how to receive. Jesus gives us more than we can imagine. He hears our cries for mercy. He cleanses us. Cleansed, we must return, throw ourselves at his feet, and give thanks.

"It is more blessed to give than to receive," Jesus said (Acts 20:35). Surely that is true if we are talking about giving to those in need. But many of us need to first learn how to receive.

Have you ever gotten an extravagant present for your birthday? Perhaps a friend you don't even know very well gives you something expensive. As you unwrap the gift, your eyes grow wide with surprise. "How nice!" is your first thought. "How can I ever pay them back?" is your second. You may not even be able to enjoy the gift for worrying about what you will give them in return.

By contrast, children know how to receive. They tear into the presents, throwing paper everywhere. "Wow! Thanks!" they say and you know they mean it. They're not contemplating what they can get you. They're enjoying what you gave them.

We need to learn how to enjoy God's gifts: by saying "Wow! Thanks!" As Christians, the gifts of money, time, and goodwill we give to others are our poor attempts to thank Jesus for what he has done for us. Like this Samaritan leper, we were outside the fold of God. Diseased, unclean, sinful. Jesus cleansed us by his blood. We can only receive this gift as unworthy sinners. We cannot repay, only thank.

Being a Christian is not a matter of being better than others or earning points with God through good works. Here is what it means to be a Christian, a child of God, one cleansed by Jesus: we are those who give thanks to God. We thank him by worship and service to him. We thank him by binding the wounds of the stranger. In each moment of each day we thank him by faithful service that expects no thanks in return.

Jesus sends out his disciples with the following instructions:

"As you go, preach this message: 'The kingdom of heaven is near.' Heal the sick, raise the dead, cleanse those who have leprosy, drive out demons. Freely you have received, freely give" (Matthew 10:7-8).

We learn from two Samaritans.
We learn how to receive.
    Freely.
We learn how to give.
    The same way.

CHAPTER FIVE

LEAVE US ALONE

Luke 8:26-39

"Then all the people . . . asked Jesus to leave them . . ." Luke 8:37.

Evil.

Do we really believe in evil anymore? A recent poll in a news magazine says many Americans today have little concept of shame. Murderers sit in courtrooms facing the families of their victims without a shred of remorse. Guilt? Our therapeutic culture tells us that guilt is only in our own mind, the result of psychological repression. Sin? It's an outmoded word. Who really sees himself as a vile sinner anymore? Isaac Watts asked, "Would He devote that sacred head for such a worm as I?" Modern hymnbooks have changed that to "such a one as I." We don't think we're worms. It's not good for our self-esteem.

If our society has lost words like "shame," "guilt," and "sin," then what do we do with "evil"? Rarely does anyone call someone or something evil. The few times I do hear it, the term is reserved for Hitler or Saddam or the current madman of the moment. "Oh sure, Hitler was evil," we think, "but we don't want to put ordinary people into the same category as Hitler." People we know may do bad things, but they're not bad people. We don't call them evil.

Evil — Then and Now

Jesus confronted evil. Real evil. Evil that made its presence clearly known.

He came to the region of the Gerasenes and was met by a demon-possessed man. The man was out-of-control, living naked among the tombs, an outcast from society. For a while, his friends in town had tried to help this man control the evil spirit. When the demon seized him, his neighbors chained him hand and foot and kept him under guard to prevent him from hurting himself and others. It did no good. He broke the chains, fled the town, and went out to live alone. No power could tame this demon.

What are we to make of this talk of demons and evil spirits? To many this sounds like primitive superstition. Early humans didn't know about seizures or psychological problems, so they explained them in terms of demons, much as they explained lightning as bolts thrown by the gods. Jesus simply accommodated himself to the times in which he lived. Like us, he knew there was no such thing as a demon.

But it's not so easy to explain away the New Testament teaching on demons. These demons talk, they cry out, they make requests. Later in this story, they are sent into pigs. Did the pigs have psychological problems? I don't think so. As much as we may hate to admit it, Jesus confronted real demons, evil spirits.

What does this mean for us today? Do demons still possess people or did that happen only in New Testament times? I'm not sure. There are stories even today of demon possession. Are they true? I can't say. What I do know is that the world is a strange and complicated place and there are more things in heaven and earth than are dreamed of in our philosophy. I also know there is evil in the world. Real unexplained evil.

Evil is the only explanation for Jeffrey Dahmer. All his acquaintances in Milwaukee thought Jeffrey was a mild-mannered young man. He wouldn't hurt a fly. But he did. He quietly waylaid seventeen people, tortured them to death, and dismembered their bodies. He even practiced cannibalism. Dahmer's true story is so horrific that the most graphic movie murderer seems tame by comparison. Dahmer's acts were not fiction. They were real.

How do we explain someone like Jeffrey Dahmer? Is it merely bad chemistry that determined his behavior? Was he just socially maladjusted? Or is there evil, palpable evil, that sometimes overcomes us? When we think of demons, of some supernatural power of evil, we find it hard to get the Hollywood version of possession out of our minds. We remember those horror movies of people with their heads turning backwards and their bodies floating off the ground. Such pictures are more laughable than horrible.

However, evil is real and it carries with it real horror. Just ask the families of these murder victims. Just ask this young man who doesn't know why he did these horrible things. Dread fills us when we think of an evil force that overcomes us against our will. I don't have all the answers about demons. I do know that demons were real in Jesus' day. I know evil is still with us. The fate of the demon-possessed man is a story for our time.

"Leave Me Alone"

Jesus gets off the boat and immediately confronts this man with the demon. Or rather demons, for later we find many demons had gone into him, so many that the demon called himself "Legion." A legion in the Roman army consisted of 4000 to 6000 soldiers. Perhaps it's not meant literally here, but even so, the man had a bunch of demons.

The demons recognize Jesus. They always do. They always recognize one who is good, one who has power over them. So the demons cry out to Jesus and say what evil always says to good, "What do you want with me, Jesus, Son of the Most High God?" (Luke 8:28). All evil ever asks good is, "Leave me alone."

Edmund Burke said, "The only thing necessary for the triumph of evil is for good men to do nothing." Evil just wants to be left alone. How easy it is for those who think they are good to ignore evil. How often have we seen injustice and turned our backs saying, "It's none of our business"? How often have we seen people in trouble, in the grip of evil, guilt, shame, and sin, and excused ourselves by thinking, "It's their life. I don't want to pry"? Do we sometimes even ignore the cries of those closest to us — husband, wife, child, parent — because they say, "Leave me alone."

Jesus wouldn't let evil alone. He wouldn't let this poor man alone. He loved him too much. So Jesus commands the demons to depart. "Why do you torture us?" they cry. When good confronts evil, evil may not see it as a blessing. When we try to help those in sin, it may take tough love. They may even see us not as helpers, but as torturers.

Have you ever tried to help someone who scorned your help? I know some teachers who did everything they could to help a student. They helped him find a place to stay, got him a scholarship to school, bought him eyeglasses, tutored him without cost, loaned him money, bailed him out of jail. What did he do? He condemned them in front of anyone who'd listen to them, accusing them of exploiting him. Those we help may see us as meddlers. They may think we mean them harm, not good. Jesus knew what that was like. He still wouldn't leave those in need alone.

Back to the story of Jeffrey Dahmer. He was found guilty of his crimes, sentenced to several consecutive life sentences, and sent to prison. At that point the good people of Milwaukee and America breathed a sigh of relief.

The monster was behind bars. The evil one was chained. Most Americans forgot Dahmer. They left him alone.

One woman would not. Mary Mott lived in Virginia, far away from Milwaukee. She'd never heard of Dahmer until she saw him on the news. Mary is a Christian who lives her faith. She heard the story of this terrible man and thought, "If anyone needs Jesus, Jeffrey Dahmer does." She not only thought it, she did something about it. She sent him a correspondence course on the Bible and salvation. She wouldn't let him alone.

Jesus will not let the demons alone. He commands them to depart, but they make a last request. "Don't send us into the Abyss," they cry, "but let us go into this nearby herd of pigs." Jesus gives permission. They enter the pigs, causing them to run off a bank and drown in the lake below.

This is the part of the story we always remember. As kids we could clearly picture the squealing, twisting pigs plummeting to their death. Some animal lovers might even blame Jesus for killing these innocent pigs. What harm had they done? Others think Jesus did this on purpose to rid the area of pig-farming. After all, pigs were unclean according to the Law. Why did these Jews raise them?

A warning: don't get hung up on the pigs. They are not the focus of the story. The story is about good and evil. About power and compassion. About a Lord who cares for those in the grip of some force they cannot understand.

Look at the man, not the pigs. This man who had no control of his life, who was out of his mind, who ran naked through the tombs, is now sitting at the feet of Jesus. Clothed. In his right mind. His life returned to him, returned by One more powerful than thousands of demons.

Evil is real. Satan "prowls around like a roaring lion looking for someone to devour" (1 Peter 5:8). He is assisted by his angels, the demons. He is the prince of this present world. But the good news is "the one who is in you is greater than the one who is in the world" (1 John 4:4). We do not fear Satan or demons or evil of any kind. Why? Because they do not exist? No, they are real, as real to us as they were to this man. No, we do not fear them because Jesus has power over them. He is not a good man who does nothing. He is the Son of the Most High who has compassion on us and casts evil out of our lives.

This man with the demons was lost. Lost in every sense of the word. He'd lost his mind. He'd lost control of himself. He'd lost contact with others. He'd lost his very humanity. Jesus finds him. Jesus casts out evil. Jesus gives him back his mind. When we are in our right mind, we find ourselves where this man was found: at the feet of Jesus.

Jeffrey Dahmer was lost. Lost in every sense of the word. But through the correspondence course he received from Mary Mott, Jeffrey saw one who had power over evil. For the first time, he saw Jesus. Jeffrey came to faith in prison and was baptized into Jesus. After his baptism, he studied the Bible to learn more of his Lord. He too was found in his right mind, seated at Jesus' feet.

Leave Us Alone

The townspeople hear of this great miracle and have to go see for themselves. They come out to Jesus and find the man clothed, in his right mind, at the feet of Jesus. What do they do? Do they shout and rejoice because God has healed this man? Do they embrace him as one who was lost but now is found? Do they fall at Jesus' feet and ask for mercy? Do they beg Jesus to come to their village and teach?

None of the above. They beg Jesus not to come but to go. They all ask him to leave the area.

Why?

Some suggest it's because of the pigs. Jesus has come and disrupted their business. They had a lot of money tied up in those pigs! Yes, it's true that they shouldn't have been raising unclean animals, but what business was that of Jesus? He should let them alone. If they didn't get rid of him, no telling what he would do next.

Perhaps the pigs had something to do with it, but that's not what Luke says. He doesn't say, "They came and saw the dead pigs and asked Jesus to leave." He says they saw the man clothed and in his right mind, and they were afraid and asked Jesus to leave.

Afraid? What were they afraid of? Afraid Jesus would kill more pigs? I don't think so. They saw this man with evil that no one could chain. Now the evil was gone. Jesus had power over demons. He had the power of goodness, of holiness. They saw the power. It scared them.

There is a word that contains both "power" and "goodness." A word our world has largely forgotten. That word is "holiness." The modern world has done more than empty holiness of its meaning; it has turned its meaning upside down. If someone at work calls you "holy," you can be sure it is not a compliment. To most folk it means hypocrite, egotist, "holier than thou."

It was not always so. Holiness is a powerful word, a biblical word we need to recover. It carries with it both the idea of moral goodness and the idea of dangerous power. In the Old Testament, the holiness of God was nothing to be trifled with. Moses is told to take off his shoes because he was on holy ground. When Israel reaches Sinai, they are warned not to get too close to the holy mountain. To do so meant sudden death.

Holiness is frightening. Near my house is a large electrical substation with row after row of transformers. As you approach it, the air begins to crackle, your hair stands on end, and you think to yourself, "This is not exactly a safe place." One doesn't have to read the warning signs on the fence around the plant to know there is danger.

It is much the same way when one approaches the holiness of God. One begins to tremble with fear. This is a God who is all good. We are not. This is a God of absolute power, dangerous power. "Warning!" the sign around him says, "The Holy One of Israel."

This is why the people see the man at Jesus' feet and react with fear. They see the Holy One. They see Jesus who is so good that his holiness drives out the greatest of demons. They see Jesus who is so powerful that his holiness conquers evil. They see Jesus and they know their own evil, their own weakness. They see it and they don't like it. They want Jesus to go away.

So he does. He will not stay in a place or in a heart that does not want him. The demons tell him, "Go away. Leave us alone." He will not go away, but stays and casts them out. The Gerasenes say, "Go away," and he goes. Why? Because there is something worse than demons, worse than evil, worse than sin. What can be worse than being a sinner? Being a sinner who won't admit your sin, who won't allow Jesus to forgive. By seeing his holiness we also see the depth of our sin. We can ignore that sin by sending him away. Without him there to remind us, our shame and guilt don't seem as bad. But they are. They rob us of our minds, our senses, our humanity. They make us lost among the tombs of contemporary culture. If we send him away, we send away our only hope.

Or our fear of Jesus can move us to fall at his feet. If we embrace his terrible holiness we also find his bottomless mercy. He casts out our demons. He clothes us in robes of righteousness. He saves.

He even saved Jeffrey Dahmer. The end of Dahmer's story is well known. Just a few weeks after he was saved, he was himself the victim of a bloody murder. Some would say he finally got what he deserved, and in terms of justice, they would be right. I believe he got more. He received mercy.

A month or so after Dahmer's death, I received a newsletter from a nationally popular Christian radio program. The newsletter assured its readers that there was something not quite theologically sound with Dahmer's baptism. The tone of the letter suggested that good Christians could rest assured that a horrible murderer like Dahmer had not stained their honorable name. Why would anyone question God's grace to Dahmer?

Fear. Fear that God's grace might really be free, free to the worst of sinners. Fear that Jesus might forgive indiscriminately. Afraid that Jesus' holiness might be smudged by saving such a one.

I believe Jesus has the power to overcome evil. Even the evil of Jeffrey Dahmer. He overcomes not by ignoring the evil, but by forgiving it. I believe Jeffrey Dahmer is my brother in Christ. I find that greatly assuring. If God saved Dahmer, he can save even me.

Go and Tell

The Gerasenes ask Jesus to leave. As he boards the boat to go, the man he saved begs to go with him. The crowd wants Jesus far away from them. The man wants him near. Jesus agrees to the demons' request. He sends them into the hogs. Jesus agrees to the crowd's request. He leaves their country. He does not grant the man's request. He sends him away.

Why? Why wouldn't Jesus let the man go with him? Why does Jesus say no to this man when he had told so many others, "Follow me"?

Because he has another plan for the man, a higher call. The Gerasenes will not allow Jesus to stay, so Jesus sends this man in his place. "'Return home and tell how much God has done for you.' So the man went away and told all over town how much Jesus had done for him" (Luke 8:39).

What do we do with evil? Do we ignore it? Pretend it isn't there? Explain it away with psychology or science?

What do we do with evil in our own lives? Convince ourselves we're not that bad, only human? Admit we make mistakes, but avoid the tough words that best describe our situation? "Shame." "Guilt." "Sin." After all, we're no worse than some people and better than most. Is that why we ignore Jesus? Is that why we're afraid of him? Is that why we even secretly hope he'll go away, because compared to others we're not that bad, but compared to him, we just don't measure up.

No. We are not among those who say to Jesus, "Please leave." We are those who admit their sin, who turn to him, who know that he alone can cast out evil from our lives.

And he did. On the cross. And he does. By his resurrection. So we sit at his feet, never wanting to leave.

But he bids us go. He wants us to go and tell. There are others around us who need to know what he has done for us. What he can do for them. So we go and tell all over our towns how much he has done for us.

Some will hear us. Then they face the test.

What do you say to Jesus?

"Leave me alone," you say.

He seeks us through long days and nights, but if we insist, he goes his way.

"Let me go with you," you say. He bids you come. Follow. Then go. Tell.

CHAPTER SIX

GO FISH!

Luke 5:1-11

"Put out into deep water, and let down the nets for a catch" Luke 5:4.

Skydiving. Mountain climbing. Auto racing. Chainsaw juggling.

What do they have in common?

All are dangerous sports. In each there is always a good chance one may lose life or limb. This possibility of injury gives these sports at least part of their appeal. In them one courts danger, living on the edge, looking death in the face and laughing.

A Dangerous Sport

What are other dangerous sports?

How about fishing?

"Fishing?" you say. "You've got to be kidding." Fishing calls forth images of lazy days beside a still lake or river. It's a relaxing pastime, a time to get away from the pressures of life. Fishing is just sitting with a pole in your hand. What could be less dangerous than that? Fishing may bring thrills, but not the thrill of facing sudden death.

Unless you're my friend Mark.

Last weekend Mark went with a friend to fish near South Padre Island. Friday night they fished almost all night for flounder. They caught nothing.

The next morning they went out on the friend's boat. Still no luck. Mark's friend, a devout Christian, was getting frustrated by their lack of success and said (half-kiddingly) "God, why did you have to scare all the fish away?"

He decided to try another spot, so off they went down the channel at about thirty miles per hour. Mark went forward to stow some life preservers. His friend at the wheel looked down to check the gas gauge, then looked up to see the bank just ahead of him.

"The next thing I knew," Mark told us later. "I was turning somersaults in the air. My first thought was 'This is it, I'm dead.'"

But he wasn't. Instead, he was hanging upside down in a mesquite tree. Falling to the ground, he felt for broken bones, found none, then stood up. Only when his ashen-faced friend ran up to him did Mark find out he'd cut his head.

Hours later at the hospital, after the stitches, it hit Mark again how close he'd come to death and how fortunate he'd been. He came home with no fish. He didn't care.

The Professional Fisherman

Fishing can be dangerous, as a sport or as a profession. There was once a group of professional fisherman who, like Mark, got more than they bargained for on their fishing expedition. In the middle of doing what they had done day after day and time after time, they suddenly ran into something more startling and surprising than a bank. They too have their world turned upside down.

It all started like an ordinary day, or rather an ordinary night. Peter and his partners, James and John, prepared their nets, got into their boats, and cast off for some night fishing. They were professional fishermen like their fathers and grandfathers before them. They knew the

Sea of Galilee like the backs of their hands, knew where the fish would be and when they would be there. They cast their nets with elegance as if they were extensions of their bodies. Then they sat in the boat to wait. They knew how to wait. They knew how to fish. This was their life.

So they waited. And waited. And waited some more. Finally John suggested they try another spot. Grunting with the effort, they pulled the nets back into the boat, cast off, and rowed. "This is where they'll be," said James. Back into the water went the nets. Back to waiting went the fisherman. They knew how to wait.

Still no fish. So they try another spot. And another. And another. Soon the sky begins to lighten. Day breaks. Still no fish.

Tired, frustrated, and disappointed, they return to shore. Dragging their boats onto land, they begin to wash and fold their nets. "We'll try again tonight," Peter says.

The Obedient Disciple

Their work is interrupted by a crowd. "What are so many people doing at the lakeside this morning?" they think. Then they spot Jesus. "Ah," they say, "so that's it. They've all come to hear the new Rabbi."

The crowd is so eager to hear Jesus, they push him to the edge of the lake. Seeing Peter's boat, he steps inside. "Simon," he says, "push the boat a little from the shore." So Simon pushes the boat and jumps in beside Jesus who teaches the people from the boat. "I never thought my boat would be a pulpit," thinks Peter.

Jesus teaches the crowd for quite some time. Peter's mind wanders from fatigue. After all, he'd been working all night. Suddenly Peter hears Jesus call his name. "What, Lord?" he says.

"I'm through teaching for today," says Jesus. "Let's go fishing. Put out in the deep water and let down your nets."

"What a time for a fishing trip!" mused Peter. "I'm sick of fishing. Besides, this Jesus is no fisherman. He's just a carpenter and a rabbi. A fishing boat is no place for a preacher. He can bless the boat, but if he comes with us he might hear some language he wouldn't hear in the synagogue. Furthermore, if we didn't catch anything all night, what makes him think he can? But he is the Teacher and he did heal my mother-in-law, so I owe him one."

So he says, "Master, we've worked hard all night and haven't caught a thing, but if you say so, I'll let down the nets."

At this point, Peter's faith is tested. Peter is a fisherman, a professional. Jesus is not. When it comes to fishing, can we blame Peter for thinking he knows more than Jesus?

Do we ever think we know more than Jesus? Do we ever accuse him of meddling in areas where he is no expert? How many of us confine our Christianity to one day, Sunday, or one place, the church? "Religion's fine," we say, "in its place." But if the preacher or Bible teacher implies that the principles of Jesus should rule our lives at work on Monday, we think they've gone too far. What does Jesus know about business? "Turn the other cheek" may work for the preacher, he doesn't live in the dog eat dog world we live in. In our world if you turn the other cheek, you just get knocked down again.

So we try to confine Jesus to the ghetto called "Religion." Just keep him there where he belongs. But our chains won't hold him. He keeps meddling in areas that don't concern him. He thinks he should be the Lord of every part of our lives. He even tries to tell Peter how to fish.

But Peter is an obedient disciple. Against his inclination and better judgment, he does what Jesus says. He lowers the nets.

What happens astounds him. Where there had been no fish the night before, there now are hundreds. The nets begin to break! "James, John, come quickly!" he shouts. With great effort they haul up the nets and fill both boats so full they begin to sink beneath the weight.

The Sinful Servant

Peter sees all this and reacts violently. Falling at the feet of Jesus, he cries, "Get away from me, Lord; I am a sinful man!"

Why such an extreme reaction? True, this is an amazing miracle, but just before this Jesus had healed Peter's mother-in-law from fever. Peter did not react so strongly then, why does he do so now?

Because Jesus has invaded Peter's home turf (or rather, home surf). When Jesus heals his mother-in-law, Peter is impressed, but after all, maybe Jesus just knows more about healing than Peter does. Peter is no physician.

He is a fisherman. He knows how and where and when to catch fish. But now Jesus has invaded his territory. Peter, James, and John had worked all night, catching nothing. They were professionals. If they caught no fish, then there were none to be caught.

Yet Jesus comes and with a word catches more fish than Peter had ever seen at one time. Suddenly Peter saw Jesus as he'd never seen him before. The power in Jesus couldn't be contained in words like "religion" or "teaching" or even "healing." It was a power over all. The power of God himself. The power of holiness.

So Peter reacts strongly. We understand that. But we expect him to say, "Lord, how powerful you are!" or "Lord, I tremble before one who can do such things." Why does he react with these words: "Depart from me, I am a sinner"? Is this just another example of Peter's impulsiveness? Does he just blurt out the first thing that comes to mind?

No. These are very appropriate words. Peter has caught a glimpse of the power of God in Jesus. He has seen Jesus for who he is: the Holy One of God. Only God himself who made the world, the sea, and all within it could call forth such a catch. Here in a small boat in a small lake in a small corner of the world is God himself. The earth cannot contain him, much less Peter's boat.

What does one do in the presence of God? Peter knows. He knows that one must bow in fear, in reverence, in the certainty that God is holy and I am not. Peter does what Isaiah does before him. Isaiah sees the Lord seated on his heavenly throne, surrounded by angels crying:

Holy, holy, holy is the Lord Almighty;
the whole earth is full of his glory.

In the presence of the thrice holy God, what does one do? Isaiah cries:

Woe to me! I am ruined! For I am a man of unclean lips, and I live among a people of unclean lips, and my eyes have seen the King, the Lord Almighty (Isaiah 6:5).

What do we do in the presence of a Holy God and a Holy Jesus? What do we do when we see Jesus where we least expect him: not at church but on our turf? When we see his power in our families, at our jobs, in school, even at play? When he muscles into those areas where we think we are professionals?

We bow. In fear, in repentance, we fall at his feet. We are ruined, for he is Holy God and we are unclean. He amazes us and scares us with what he has done, what he can do.

The Fisher of Men

And what does Jesus do with one who falls before him and admits his sins? He does what God did to Isaiah.

He cleanses, he strengthens, he calls, he sends. An angel touches Isaiah's lips with a coal and proclaims, "See, this has touched your lips; your guilt is taken away and your sin is atoned for" (Isaiah 6:7). God then calls for one to go for him. Isaiah responds: "Here am I. Send me!" The Lord sends him forth with a message for his people.

Peter's story is the same. He falls at Jesus' feet, a sinner. He is raised by Jesus with the words "Don't be afraid; from now on you will catch men" (Luke 5:10). The forgiveness Jesus gives frees Peter from the bondage and fear sin brings. It frees him to hear the call to catch others.

"Catching people" is a strange term for evangelism. After all, we catch fish for our own good, not the good of the fish. But the Greek word for "catch" here means "to capture alive." Peter is called not to bring death to fish, but to bring life to people. This metaphor of fishing for proclaiming God's will is therefore not so strange. It also has its roots in the Old Testament prophets, although there it usually is a picture of God's judgment on evil.

God warns his people through Jeremiah, "But now I will send for many fishermen, and they will catch them" (Jeremiah 16:16). They are caught for judgment: "I will repay them double for their wickedness and their sin . . ."(Jeremiah 16:18).

Amos repeats the warning:

The Sovereign Lord has sworn by his holiness:
   "The time will surely come
when you will be taken away with hooks,
   the last of you with fishhooks" (Amos 4:2).

In the Old Testament it is an awful thing to be caught by God, caught like a fish with a hook. To be a prophet, a fisher of people, was a horrible calling, for it meant one pronounced the judgment of God on his people.

Peter's call is different. The one who calls him came into the world not "to condemn the world, but to save the world . . ."(John 3:17). He hooks men not to clean them for eating, but to clean them from sin. He rescues them alive from the deep waters of guilt and despair.

Peter, James, and John are called to this task of fishing for men. They hear the call, but it is not without cost. They pull their boats to shore, then leave everything to follow Jesus.

It's a disturbing picture. "They left everything and followed him." They leave two boats full of fish for other workers to clean. They had worked all night for fish and gotten nothing. Now they have more fish than they can imagine and they leave it all behind. They leave fish and family and profession and all that is familiar to them to follow this stranger. Why? Because in him they have seen more than fish, more than family, more than familiarity and comfort. They have seen power. They have seen holiness. They have seen God.

Our Call to Catch People

My friend Mark found out that fishing can be dangerous. Peter, James and John do too. They go out on the boat expecting nothing, not even fish. On that boat their world turns topsy-turvy, head-over-heels, upside down. They go to catch fish. Jesus goes to catch them. He gets what he came for. They return to shore changed men, looking for people not fish.

We too are called to fish for people, to capture them alive for Jesus. We call it evangelism. No word frightens Christians more than "evangelism." Why does it frighten us? Perhaps it reminds us of older evangelism techniques — knocking on doors, passing out tracts, busing people in — that didn't work. Perhaps it reminds us of times we tried to share our faith and came away embarrassed. Perhaps it seems to us like meddling to question the spiritual state of others. Perhaps it's just too hard. We don't want to do it.

What will move us to overcome our fear of evangelism? Only a greater fear. Peter sees the great catch of fish that comes at Jesus' command. It scares him to death. It scares him because he is in the presence of the power of God. What will move us to catch people? Fear. Fear of Jesus. Not the fear he will condemn us if we don't evangelize, but that holy fear that sees him as he is. If we but glimpse his power in every moment of our lives, then nothing else can scare us. If we hear his voice say, "Don't be afraid," then we are ready to tell others of his grace. If we hear his command, "Go, catch people," then we know he gives us the power to reel them in.

Here is our greatest obstacle to evangelism: we try to do it by ourselves. We trust in our own abilities or in the latest techniques to get the job done, or we leave evangelism to the professionals, to preachers. Like the disciples we have toiled all night on our own; we've tried to make disciples, but we have failed. We fail because we do not rely on the one who bids us, "Put out into deep water, and let down your nets."

We must cast our nets for people. To do so requires effort. It may even require sleepless nights of toil. It requires we leave everything, as these disciples did. It requires we risk ridicule, embarrassment, and hurt feelings to share the gospel.

We must cast our nets for people, but we rely not on our own abilities for success. We rely on the powerful Lord. Sometimes we may not know where to cast. The Lord may call those whom we consider the least likely converts. We must cast where he leads. At times we may grow discouraged at our lack of success. We may go days, weeks, and months without a nibble. We should never be discouraged, knowing that we are faithful disciples. We are obedient disciples who launch into the deep at the command of our Lord, knowing he came to catch people.

Not with a hook, but with a cross.

CHAPTER SEVEN

JUST DROPPED IN

Luke 5:17-26

"We have seen remarkable things today" Luke 5:26.

Last night on the news I saw another story about yet another lawsuit. Litigation seems to be our national pastime. In this case, a group of disabled citizens was suing a local video chain for not providing handicapped access to their stores, as is mandated by the Americans with Disabilities Act.

"Another lawsuit," I thought, "just what our country needs. Another excuse for lawyers to get rich while companies and taxpayers get fleeced."

Then I thought again. Perhaps this lawsuit had merit. What would it be like to be disabled, to be chained (as it were) to a wheelchair? To be robbed of abilities that most of us don't even think about. The ability to go where we want, do what we want. The ability to work. Even the ability to wash and shave and feed ourselves. What must it be like to be at the mercy of family or friends or strangers? Wouldn't we want as much independence as we could get? Is it too much to ask that we be allowed to enter public places of business like everyone else?

Like you, I have friends and acquaintances who are wheelchair bound. Most of the time I don't even notice because they are so adept at coping with their situation. But at times they must ask for help. They must rely on others. Sometimes, even with help, it's not easy for them to get where they need to go.

A Man with Problems

There was a man who had a problem. Three problems to be exact.

For one, he was paralyzed. He couldn't move his hands and arms. An accident had stolen his normal life from him and for years he had to count on others. Unable to move. Unable to care for himself. He had to rely on his friends to bathe him, shave him, feed him, and to take him anywhere he needed to go.

That was his second problem. He had heard a healer was coming to town, a rabbi named Jesus. This Jesus was rumored to have amazing powers. He had healed lepers, the lame, and the blind. The paralyzed man felt something he hadn't felt for years: hope. Hope that this Jesus could make him well, that his life would be normal again. But how could he get to Jesus? He knew the house where he was teaching, but he couldn't get there.

A Man with Friends

Enter his four friends. They grab the corners of his bedroll and carry him to the house. He's fairly heavy; their arms strain with the effort, but they walk with smiles on their faces, knowing the rabbi will make their friend walk again.

Then they face the third problem, the insurmountable one. The crowd is too large. It fills the house, spills out into the street, and blocks their way. "Excuse us." "Pardon." "Can we squeeze by?" they say, but it's no use, they can't get in. Their friend is doomed to a lifetime of paralysis. "Well, at least we tried," one thinks. "No one can accuse us of not caring about our friend."

Then another one of them looks up. "There's more than one way to skin a cat," he says as he points to the roof. The others look puzzled, but then understand. They manhandle their friend onto the roof, bed and all. One goes to find some rope. He returns and ties the rope to the corners of the bed, while the other three begin to dig through the baked clay.

Inside the house, Jesus is teaching. Caleb, the owner of the house, is as proud as he can be. The Master had agreed to come home with him, and what is more, the news had spread throughout the countryside. The greatest scholars of the law from Galilee, Judea, and Jerusalem had come to hear Jesus. Here they sat in Caleb's house! He could hardly believe it. "I must be the most envied man in the village today," he thought to himself.

Still, he hadn't figured on such a large crowd. They trampled his carpets, sat in the windows and doors, and pressed in so close one could hardly breathe. Funny though, Jesus didn't seem to mind the crowd, for he taught them and healed them with goodwill and patience.

Suddenly Caleb's musings are interrupted by a sound above him. Surely the crowd hadn't spilled over onto his roof. Jesus looks up too, but continues with his teaching.

Then they hear a scratching sound above them. "Mighty loud mice you have there, Caleb," Jesus says with a smile. Caleb returns an embarrassed smile, thinking "What in the world can be going on?"

The scratching gets louder. "Maybe it's not mice, but goats you have up there, eh Caleb?"

Then the ceiling begins to cave in, showering Jesus and the other teachers with dust. Jesus takes it in stride, but some of the Pharisees look sternly at their host. Caleb is mortified.

Soon great chunks of clay rain down on their heads. Sunlight streams in and a face appears above them, then two, then three, then four.

"What's happening?" thinks Caleb. "Who's doing this to me, ruining what was the greatest day of my life?"

Suddenly all eyes turn upward as something descends into the room. "It's a man," someone whispers. "It's the one who is paralyzed," shouts another. Some in the crowd are amused. What a sight, to see a man on a mat lowered into a room by four ropes. Others hold their breath with anticipation. Many in the room are Pharisees, experts in the Law. They know their Bibles. They know that when the lame walk, the kingdom of God is near. As Isaiah said:

> Then will the eyes of the blind be opened
> > and the ears of the deaf be unstopped.
> Then will the lame leap like a deer,
> > and the mute tongue shout for joy.
> Water will gush forth in the wilderness
> > and streams in the desert (Isaiah 35:5-6).

So they wait to see what this Jesus will do. They wait to see if the kingdom has come.

The paralyzed man comes to rest at Jesus' feet. Jesus looks at him. He is not amused, but amazed. He marvels at the faith of the man's friends. What friends these must be, refusing to be defeated. Not settling for just a good effort, they found a way against all odds to bring the man to the healer. Jesus knows the crowd waits to see if the lame will leap. So Jesus gives the man what he needs.

A Man with a Savior

You see, the man had another problem. A problem far worse than pain, lack of mobility, or the press of the crowd. Jesus knew that problem.

"Friend, your sins are forgiven you."

"What is Jesus doing?" think some in the crowd. "The man needs healing, not forgiving. Make him walk, then worry about his sins."

The Pharisees and teachers of the law are shocked. They can't believe their ears! Does this Jesus really believe he has the power to forgive sins? God alone can forgive! Does this Rabbi, this carpenter from Nazareth believe he is God?

"Blasphemy! Blasphemy!" they cry. But only to themselves. Jesus is so popular with the crowd that they fear to say it out loud.

But Jesus knows what they're thinking.

"What makes you think these things?" he asks. "You've sat here and heard my teaching without correcting me. You've seen me heal person after person. Where do you think that teaching and that power come from? It can only come from God. If he gives me power to heal men's bodies, don't you think he gives me power to heal men's souls?"

So turning to the paralyzed man, Jesus says, "Get up, take your mat and go home."

The man begins to stir. The crowd gasps as he stands upright. He rolls up his mat, tucks it under his arm, and presses through the crowd. Praising God at the top of his lungs, he reaches the door. Tumbling down the stairs from the roof come his friends. He embraces them. Shoulder to shoulder they walk down the road toward home.

A day like no other day. This man regains his life. The friends see their loyalty rewarded beyond their dreams. The crowds see spectacle after spectacle. Teaching, healing, a man lowered through a roof, sins forgiven. They all go home saying, "We've seen remarkable things today."

Supporting Cast

An amazing day. An amazing story. Where do you find yourself in the story? Which character do you relate to?

Perhaps we identify with the friends. Few things in life are as deeply rewarding as true and lasting friendship.

What is a friend? One with whom we can laugh or cry or talk or be silent. With a friend you can be yourself. You don't have to pretend. You can share any thought, any feeling without fear. A friend gives warmth and strength.

More than anything, a true friend is someone you can count on. Friendship isn't tested until hard times come. "A friend loves at all times, and a brother is born for adversity" (Proverbs 17:17). I have friends thousands of miles away who would be on a plane at a moment's notice if I needed them. They'd clean out their savings and give it to me. They might even donate a kidney if the tissue matched. I'd do the same for them.

I hope you have such friends too. Friends like this paralyzed man had. They left their work behind, braved the crowd, risked ridicule, and even dug through a roof to help their friend. Would we do the same?

A story of true friendship.

Or maybe we relate best to the host in whose house this occurs. He's not a major character in the Bible story. He's not even named (I called him "Caleb"). However, there was such a man who had his house overrun with Pharisees and teachers of the law and common people and the sick. All to see Jesus. Was this host proud? Was he angry at the inconvenience? Was he a disciple? We don't know. We do know he opened his house to Jesus and got more than he bargained for: a hole in the roof, a religious controversy, an amazing miracle. It's always dangerous to open the door to Jesus. You don't know what will happen.

Certainly we don't relate to the Pharisees. Or do we? The Pharisees were willing to accept Jesus as a fellow teacher of the Law. They are even willing to grant that he is a wonder-worker, a healer, one who does amazing miracles. They'd seen them with their own eyes. All this is fine. Jesus can teach the law and heal the sick and draw great crowds.

But he goes too far. He tells the paralytic, "Your sins are forgiven."

Suppose you visit a new church on Sunday. You sing. You pray. The service is no different from many you've been too. Suddenly a deacon announces, "If any of you want to confess your sins, please come forward and the pastor will forgive you." What would you think? "I must have misunderstood," you say to yourself. "He must have meant to say, 'Come forward, confess to God, and the pastor will help reassure you that God has heard your prayer.'" So you go to the deacon for clarification. He tells you, "I meant exactly what I said. Our pastor has the power to forgive sins."

Would you join that church? Would you even go back there again?

I don't think so, unless you went back to straighten them out. We are appalled that anyone would have the gall to think they can forgive sin. It's blasphemy. We can forgive those who sin against us. Only God can forgive when we sin against him.

That's exactly what the Pharisees said. Jesus forgives the paralytic's sins. Only God can forgive sin. Jesus therefore is either a blasphemous egomaniac claiming to be God or he is, in fact, God in the flesh. The Pharisees believed the first alternative. They were wrong.

Surely we are not like them. We are Christians. We confess Jesus as the Son of God, God incarnate. We know he can forgive sins. We rely on him to forgive ours.

But do we realize the enormity of that belief? Or, like the Pharisees, do we practically limit Jesus? He is our teacher. We feel comfortable with that. He heals the sick. We like that. Jesus is our friend. He is close to us. He knows how we feel because he suffered as we do. He too is human. We may forget he is much more. He is God, with all of God's holiness, justice, and wrath, as well as mercy. His ways are not our ways and we must approach him in reverence. Otherwise, like these Pharisees, we make him less than what he is.

The Hero of the Story

We learn many lessons from this miracle. We learn about friendship. What it costs. What it can accomplish. We learn about hospitality. Surprising things can happen when you open your house to strangers. We learn about blindness. The Pharisees were spiritually blind to who Jesus was: the Son of God.

We also learn about faith. The paralytic had enough faith to want to get to Jesus and be healed. His friends had faith enough to carry him to the house. They had even more faith to dig through the roof and lower the man at Jesus' feet. "When Jesus saw their faith, he said, 'Friend, your sins are forgiven'" (Luke 5:20). May we have such faith.

In learning the lessons of friendship, fellowship, and faith, we must not lose sight of the true hero of this story. At the center of the miracle is not the host, the friends, the Pharisees, or even the paralyzed man. At the center is Jesus. He is the hero of this story. Of every New Testament story. Of our story.

The point of this story? Jesus forgives sins. The greatest miracle performed that day was not the healing of one who was paralyzed, it was the forgiveness of a sinner. This is what we must learn.

Jesus saves. It's an old lesson to most of us, so old we take it for granted. "Jesus saves." We see these words emblazoned on T-shirts, in neon on billboards, and handwritten on signs at football games. They are old words. Church words. Religious words.

We know Jesus saves. We have been saved. Perhaps in our youth, in a revival, or in someone's home. Jesus saves. But what real difference does that make in our lives? We still feel depressed. Still have marriage problems. Still fight and bicker and nag. Still face boredom and failure. Still long for more. We try to help ourselves with seminars and exercise and books and vitamins and vacations and shopping. Nothing works.

Jesus saves. Not **saved**, but **saves**. Our salvation is not just something we experienced long ago; it is an ever present reality. His touch is as much in our lives now as it was on the day we accepted him as Lord. He said to the paralytic, "Your sins are forgiven." He said the same to us. He continues to say it, each moment of each day.

Sin. That is our root problem. Not boredom, depression, bad relationships, and poor self-esteem. Sin.

Worse than paralysis. Worse than any disease, it grabs hold of our lives, paralyzes our will, and immobilizes our best intentions. This man needed healing. He needed to walk. Jesus says, "Stand up and take your bed and go home." It wasn't enough. He needed something more. He needed forgiveness.

We've looked at the powerful miracles of Jesus. We've watched him make the blind see, the leper clean, the paralyzed walk. What is more, we see his power in our lives today. We take all our problems to Jesus. Our nagging illnesses. Our deepest longings. Our broken relationships. We can witness to his healing power. A sister is in the hospital with inoperable cancer. We pray. The cancer disappears. Friends have a troubled marriage, headed for divorce. We pray. They stay together. We awake and feel unable to face another day. We pray. Jesus gives us strength.

We pray. Jesus hears. We see his power. At times it comes in the form of healing. At times in the form of inner strength. Paul prays three times to the Lord to remove his thorn in the flesh. Jesus does not heal him, but he gives him what he needs: "My grace is sufficient for you . . ."(2 Corinthians 12:9).

How many times do we see the problems in our lives — financial worries, poor health, depression, lack of friendship — and go to Jesus for help? Surely he has promised to give us what we need. We must fight the paralysis that keeps us from going to him. We must overcome the crowd, overcome any obstacle that stands in the way. We must dig through any barrier that separates us from him. But do we sometimes fail to see our greatest need? Do we fail to see his greatest gift?

"Your sins are forgiven."

That's just what we need to hear.

CHAPTER EIGHT

LEAST LIKELY

John 5:1-15; Matthew 15:21-28

"Send her away, for she keeps crying out after us" Matthew 15:23.

Last night. Supper time. The phone rings.

"Mr. Holloway?" the voice asks.

I think, "Whatever you're selling, I'm not interested," but I say, "Yes."

"Mr. Holloway, I'm calling on behalf of the local chapter of the Society for the Blind. We're having our annual fund drive and could use your help."

"I'm sorry," I say, "but I don't give over the phone."

The dial tone sounds in my ear before I can finish.

Later I reflect on the conversation and begin to feel bad. After all, I'm a Christian, a minister even. I recently wrote about the compassion Jesus had for the blind. Shouldn't I help them too?

The problem is that there are too many groups that want my help. Two or three times a week I get calls like this asking me to help the handicapped, send underprivileged kids to the circus, protect battered wives, and build low-cost housing for the homeless. So I've made a policy. I never give in response to phone solicitations.

Then there are the letters. It seems I am on the mailing list of every charitable group in America. I don't send money to them all, but I do to some. The problem is deciding who to help if I can't help them all.

Every church faces the same dilemma. Few days go by without someone visiting or calling the church, looking for financial help. We want to assist as many people as we can, but we have limited resources. How do we decide to give or not to give? As individuals or churches, we must have some criteria we use to determine who is most worthy of our funds. Do we base our generosity on need? How can we tell who is neediest? Do we base it on moral considerations? Do we help those who suffer through no fault of their own but refuse aid to the able-bodied who can work for themselves? Do we base it on attitude? Do we give to the humble supplicant, but turn away the arrogant empty-handed? Worst of all, do we base it on race or gender, giving only to "our own kind"?

Jesus must have faced similar questions. Many in his day were ill, diseased, and disabled. He couldn't touch them all. He didn't heal them all. How did he decide who should be healed? We don't know. It was his sovereign choice. The faith of the sick person had something to do with it. So did their willingness to ask. Even their national origin mattered, as we will see later. But the bottom line is: Jesus healed whomever he willed.

Sometimes he heals those who are the least likely candidates for healing. Let's look at two of them. One surprises us with his pettiness. The other surprises even Jesus with her faith. The amazing thing is that Jesus gave both the help they needed.

No One to Help

He seems like the biggest jerk in the Bible.

Perhaps that's a harsh assessment, but it's the way he looks to me. He first appears as an object of pity. For thirty-eight years he had been paralyzed. Imagine. Unable to move. Dependent on others for help. Not able to do anything for yourself.

Each morning, for thirty-eight years, he had drifted out of sleep and for a moment forgotten his problem. If only for a moment, he was in his old life where he could jump, and play, and be like everyone else. Then reality set in. He would wake fully and know that his living nightmare continued. But he wouldn't give up hope, at least not completely, for each day he would nag and beg until his brother or his sister or one of his friends would carry him to the magical pool. There he would sit, waiting for it to happen.

And it did. Perhaps a dozen times in his thirty-eight years the pool's water began to mysteriously move. Each time he would drag himself toward the water, but always too late. Someone always beat him there. They were healed. He was not.

So he gave up hope. Oh, he still went to the pool, but he didn't expect anything to happen. Even if the water moved, he'd never make it in time. There was no one to help him.

Until the day a stranger came by.

"Do you want to be healed?" the stranger said.

"What do you think, stupid?" the paralytic thought. But he said with a sigh, "No one will help me, so someone else always gets into the water before I do."

"Get up and walk," the stranger said.

It had to be the strangest thing the man had ever heard. "Get up and walk" indeed. Didn't this stranger know that was why he was at the pool in the first place? "Still, it won't hurt to try," he thought.

"Get up and walk," Jesus said.

So he did.

For the first time in thirty-eight years, he stood up. He grabbed his mat and headed for home, not taking the time to thank the stranger or even find out his name.

Then he got in trouble.

"You, there," a man said, "what do you think you're doing?"

"Huh?" said the former paralytic.

"Don't you know it's against the law to carry your mat like that on the Sabbath?"

"But the man told me to."

"What man?"

"The man that healed me. You remember me, don't you? I'm the one at the pool, the one who's been paralyzed for years."

"So, who is this who healed you on the Sabbath and told you to break the law?"

"I don't know."

And so he didn't. Until Jesus found him again in the temple and warned him that there was something worse than paralysis. "Don't sin anymore or something worse may happen to you," Jesus said. So the man learned the name of his healer.

Did he stop and thank Jesus? Did he confess himself a sinner and ask Jesus to forgive? Did he proclaim to others what Christ had done for him? Did he invite him home with him?

No.

What did he do? He told on him! Going back to the Jews who had accused him of breaking the law, the healed man said, "I've got the name of the culprit now, the one who doesn't respect the Sabbath. His name is Jesus."

So they began to persecute Jesus and even tried to kill him.

What an ingrate! What a jerk! Nine of the ten lepers neglect to thank Jesus for their cleansing. We can't imagine such ingratitude. This man is even worse. Thirty-eight years without hope, he repays Jesus for his unspeakable gift by shifting the blame to him and endangering his life. He bites the hand that feeds and chews vigorously.

How do we feel about such a man? I for one am encouraged by this jerk. He was the least likely person to be helped by Jesus. He was bitter. He was self-centered. He lacked faith. He didn't know Jesus before or even after he was healed. Jesus healed him anyway.

So in our bitterest moments, our most selfish times, our most ungrateful days, Jesus can and does heal us too. We least deserve his power and his forgiveness. Out of his compassion and grace, he still freely gives.

But the healing comes with a warning: "Sin no more." We must not remain as this jerk, repaying Jesus' kindness with indifference and persecution. He has awakened us from the nightmare of our paralysis of sin, and we must learn his name, fall down at his feet in gratitude, and serve him evermore.

An Unexpected Delight

I grew up in Atlanta, Georgia and later my wife and I lived there for six years.

I hate driving in Atlanta.

I love so many things about my home city, but the traffic is absolutely deplorable. With a heavy feeling of dread I embarked on the long drive across town to pick up a friend at the Atlanta airport.

I entered the ramp to the interstate highway. Nervous, tense, looking in every direction, I entered the traffic hoping the nut behind me would slow down.

Then it happened. I looked up. Ahead of me over the city skyline was the most glorious sunset I had ever seen. It's impossible to describe a sunset, but his one placed multicolored streaks in the air amid thin swirling clouds, a scene more delicate and beautiful than any painting in any gallery in the world.

An unexpected delight.

So I traveled on, my worries gone, my body somehow lighter. I seemed to float along the highway.

It can happen with people too.

For twelve years I taught Bible in Christian high schools. Kids are forced to be in high school. They don't want to be there. Even the few who want to be there and want to learn usually act like they hate school because it's the thing to do.

One day, I was in a funk. I had been discussing something important in my classes, something that should move the heart of any human being in existence. My students didn't care. All they could think of was how their hair looked, or how cute their new boyfriend was, or how they could get tickets to the next rock concert. In despair I stopped class early, inwardly remembering the warning Jesus gave about casting pearls before swine.

Then it happened. An unexpected delight.

On my desk was a note. I opened it and read:

> *Dear Dr. Holloway,*
>   *Thanks so much for all you try to teach us. You've really made me think of things I never thought of before. You and Mrs. Holloway are very special to me.*
>

Love,
Susan.

In eleven years of teaching, I'd only had a handful of such notes. Each was like the sunset, totally unsuspected, totally uplifting.

Jesus must have had his discouraging moments too. No one wanted to listen to him. Oh, they wanted something from him all right, loaves and fish, healing, political freedom, but they didn't really want to hear what he said. They wanted to have their desires met without effort on their part, without the risk of faith. Jesus' pupils, the Jews, were with him daily, but they really didn't want to learn, to understand, to believe.

People like the man at the pool must have discouraged Jesus. Here is one who received the kindness of Jesus and repaid him with evil. We can't imagine how Jesus must have felt. As Son of God he came down to earth to seek and save the lost only to find that few wanted to be found or saved. Some repaid his love with indifference. Some with curses. Some even crucified him.

Still he continued to seek, to save, to heal, to teach.

One day Jesus' classroom was invaded by one who was not even enrolled as a pupil. A Canaanite, and a woman at that, she wanted her daughter healed. Jesus' pupils, the disciples, told him to send her away. She bothered them. So he did, saying "God sent me only to the lost sheep of Israel."

Still she persisted. "Lord, help me!" she cried.

Jesus told her she did not belong. "It is not right to take the children's bread and give it to the dogs."

"Yes, Lord," she said, "but even the dogs eat the crumbs that fall from their master's table."

Jesus was shocked, surprised. He proclaimed her his star pupil. "Woman, you have great faith!" He healed her daughter.

Jesus had found a sunset, a Susan, an unexpected pleasure.

Sometimes those we least expect have the greatest faith. Sometimes the least likely candidate becomes the greatest leader. Like Jesus, we must not be afraid to associate with those on the margins of society. We might just be surprised with an unexpected pleasure, a great faith.

Who Do We Help?

This woman is truly needy. She is unselfish. She asks not for herself, but her daughter. She is persistent, so much so that the disciples get tired of hearing her. She asks humbly, on her knees. She seems the perfect candidate for Jesus' charity.

She does not qualify. She fails to meet the ethnic requirement for help. She is not of Israel. The disciple's words to her are harsh, "Lord, send her away." Jesus sounds even harsher. He calls her a dog. How could Jesus be so insensitive? Didn't he know he'd hurt her feelings?

Yes, but Jesus cared more for truth than for hurt feelings. He was the Jewish Messiah. While here in the flesh, he was sent only to the house of Israel. Pagans like this woman had no promise of the Messiah's help.

Yet she surprises Jesus by grasping a promise not yet made. Later Paul would proclaim that the Gentiles by faith receive the same promise of the Messiah as the Jews. This woman jumps the gun on that proclamation. No wonder Jesus says, "Woman, you have great faith!" (Matthew 15:28).

On the other hand, the man at the pool is a Jew. He also is truly needy. But he doesn't even ask Jesus to make him well. He is bitter. He is resentful. Later we find him ungrateful and disloyal to Jesus.

Would we help either one?

Jesus heals them both.

What were Jesus' criteria for helping them? Was it racial? The woman was not a Jew. He heals her anyway. Was it moral? Jesus doesn't ask if they brought illness on themselves because of immorality. Was it the manner in which they ask? The woman is humble. The man is not. He heals both.

So what do these two have in common? Nothing. Nothing except their need. Both needed the power of Jesus. Both receive. The single criterion Jesus uses to determine who receives his healing touch is this: Do they need help?

"Wait a minute," we say, "that can't be right. If Jesus had helped everyone in need then he would have healed everyone in the world."

Didn't he? No. Not all the paralyzed walked. Not all the children were cured. He was sent only to Israel. He didn't cure all physical illness in his day, nor will he in ours. Still he heals all. Those who did not feel the touch of his hand still can feel the touch of his cross. He died not only for the deserving, the humble, and the righteous. He died for the undeserving. He died for sinners. He died for me. For you. We can do nothing to deserve his love. We can only rejoice in it and pledge with his help to keep his command: "Go and sin no more."

What does this say about our own giving? If Jesus gives to all, shouldn't we? Like Jesus in the days of his flesh, we can only be one place at a time. Our resources are limited. We can't give to everyone, so we must make hard decisions. We must give wisely, knowing that our money may not hurt, it may harm.

The good news is we know the One who has unlimited resources, the Great Physician who heals all by his own blood. We cannot give to all, but in our giving we must point to the One who gives without limit. Whenever we give money, time, a kind word, and a helpful hand, we do it in his name. We tell good news: Jesus saves. He takes our efforts, however feeble, and endows them with his grace.

So what do we do the next time the phone rings and someone asks for help? We help them. Perhaps we cannot give them money or volunteer our time, but we can say a prayer for them and ask God to bless. We won't wipe out sickness or poverty. The poor are always with us. However, we must do what we can, even if it's only a cup of water we give. Jesus said,

"And if anyone even gives a cup of cold water to one of these little ones because he is my disciple, I tell you the truth, he will certainly not lose his reward" (Matthew 10:42).

Two people come to Jesus. Both are needy. Neither deserve his help. Still he heals them. He helps them. He helps not because of who they are, but because he is who he is.

People come to us for help. They may not deserve it. Still we help them, not because of who they are, but because of who we are. We are disciples of Christ. We follow the one who went about doing good, who fed and healed and comforted, who saves all. We give because he gave.

The question we face with those in need is not who, or how long, or how much to help. The question is how. We help with food, money, and jobs. We help best by pointing them to the one who gives without measure. We give the good news about the one who gave himself for all.

We give them Jesus.

CHAPTER NINE

ARE YOU HUNGRY?

Mark 8:14-21

"Why are you talking about having no bread?" Mark 8:17.

Suddenly it appears on the screen, larger than life. Thick caramel topped with peanuts. Your mouth begins to water. You've ignored your hunger all day. You can ignore it no longer.

Then comes a molten river of chocolate slowly covering the bar from end to end. To top it all is a jingle, "The snack that really satisfies."

I don't even like candy bars, but if I'm hungry enough and the ad is enticing enough, I can't resist.

On television, billboards, radio, and magazines, we see them every day, hundreds of thousands of them in a lifetime: advertisements. They show us what will fill our hunger. They tell us what satisfies.

If your stomach is growling, the food ads do their work. However, it's not only our physical hungers they propose to fill. Indeed many of us don't know what it's like to be hungry. We've never gone more than a day and seldom more than a few hours without food. We do, however, know other hungers.

Have you ever had "new car fever"? Now that's a hunger! Your old car still runs well, but you do have to take it to the shop from time to time. So you convince yourself you need a new one. The true problem is your car is old; that is, it has lost its power to thrill, to excite. All the joy of driving has been emptied from it. The ads know this, so they promise excitement in the shape of a new car with more style, more features, and (what they want you to ignore) more cost. Still you buy the new car. Why? It promises to really satisfy.

Commercials promise to satisfy all our hungers, even our deepest needs. Are you lonely? The right toothpaste, perfume, or deodorant will bring people close. Are you worried about the future? Just grab a piece of the rock and you'll have peace of mind. Kids doing poorly in school? The latest video series will give them straight A's. Advertising not only promises to satisfy our old needs, it even creates hunger for new products we never knew we needed. "New and improved" is its motto.

What would starving children from other parts of the world think if they suddenly found themselves in our living rooms? How could they fathom a culture where food is plentiful, but people are never satisfied? How could they understand our "hungers" when their hunger is so pressing? They hunger for food. A little bread will satisfy. It will even save their lives.

Feeding the Hungry

Jesus knew what it was like to be hungry. Really hungry. He felt compassion for the hungry, so he fed them.

On one occasion, Jesus wanted to get away with his disciples. This was to be a retreat for them, a time of rest. The crowd that followed Jesus had other plans. They found out where Jesus was going and beat him there. We know what it's like to need to get away for awhile. How wonderful it would be to have a Saturday by ourselves! We also know how irritated we get when people interrupt our time alone.

Jesus is not irritated. He arrives and sees the crowd. Another man might have sent them away. After all, they were interfering with his plans for a quiet getaway. But Jesus had compassion on them, for they struck him as sheep without a shepherd. They needed guidance. They were hungry for direction in their lives.

So Jesus began to teach them what they needed to hear. He teaches long past supper time. The disciples come to Jesus with a suggestion: "Lord, you'd better dismiss the crowd so they can go into the surrounding villages and buy food."

Jesus startles them by saying, "No, you give them something to eat."

"Lord, it would cost eight months' wages to feed this mob! Should we spend all we have on them?"

"How much food do you have?"

"Five loaves and two fish."

"Tell the people to get ready to eat."

We know the story. He blessed the loaves and broke them. The fish also. The people ate and were satisfied. The leftovers filled twelve baskets. Jesus satisfied the hunger of five thousand with five loaves and two fish, with more left over than what he started with. Jesus knew what it was like to be hungry, so he fed the hungry.

An amazing miracle. Particularly amazing because a few days later it happened again. Another crowd gathers to hear Jesus. They follow him for three days and run out of food. Jesus calls his disciples and asks, "What should I do? If I send them home hungry, some will collapse on the way."

What do the disciples say? What would you say? How about, "Lord, why don't you do one of those food miracles like you did a few days ago?"

That's not what the disciples say. They still don't get it. They say, "We're out here in the middle of nowhere. Where can we get enough bread to feed this crowd?"

"How many loaves do you have?" Jesus asks.

"Seven, and a few fish."

95

"Get the crowd ready to eat."

So Jesus takes the loaves and fish, blesses them, breaks them, and gives them to the crowd. Four thousand people have their hunger satisfied. This time the leftovers fill seven baskets.

Immediately afterward, the Pharisees ask Jesus for a sign from heaven! How big a sign do they want? Isn't feeding nine thousand people with a few loaves enough for them? But the Pharisees don't understand. Neither do the disciples. Jesus knew what it was like to be hungry, so he satisfied the hungry.

How to Be Hungry

Jesus was hungry. Really hungry. For forty days he'd had nothing to eat. Soon the very rocks around him began to look like loaves of bread.

"Hm," he thought, "why not?" After all, he had the power to turn the stones to bread. Nice, warm bread that would melt in your mouth. He could taste it already. What would be wrong with turning the stones to bread? After all, he was the Son of God. He had made the stones at the beginning. He could remake them now.

Then he realized that was the voice of the devil. To use his power to serve his own selfish needs, even a need as real as this one, would be to betray his purpose on earth. He came to serve, not to be served. If he took the easy path now, what would he do when the going really got rough?

"No," he said. "There are things more important than my immediate need. More important than the bread that sure would taste good." He remembered the Scripture: "Man does not live on bread alone, but on every word that comes from the mouth of God" (Matthew 4:4) He would forget the bread and rely on God alone.

It seems a strange temptation. None of us are tempted to turn stone to bread. Or are we? Are we not, like Jesus, tempted often to put our immediate needs above our call to service, suffering, and obedience? When we suffer from hunger, from doubt, from pain, from loneliness, do we expect God to immediately make things right? Do we think, "Surely he doesn't intend for his children to suffer?"

But he does. He wants us to suffer for our own good. The Bible passage Jesus quotes in this temptation begins:

> Remember how the Lord your God led you all the way in the desert these forty years, to humble you and to test you in order to know what was in your heart, whether or not you would keep his commands. He humbled you, causing you to hunger and then feeding you with manna, which neither you nor your fathers had known, to teach you that man does not live on bread alone but on every word that comes from the mouth of the LORD (Deuteronomy 8:2-3).

God shows his love to Israel by giving them bread. He shows it even more by testing their obedience. He wants them to want him more than they want bread. Jesus faces the same test. Did God want Jesus to be hungry? I think he did. To teach him that there's something more important than immediate gratification. After all, resisting temptation always means imposing limits on our desires and appetites. Or rather it means exchanging one hunger for a better one. We hunger not for bread, but hunger and thirst for righteousness (Matthew 5:6). Jesus learned it was God, not bread, that sustains life. Have we learned?

As a child, I sometimes fumed at my parents because they were so cruel. They didn't give me everything I wanted! Looking back, I'm awfully glad they didn't. "But I *need* it, Momma." What would you think of a mother who gives in to her child's every whim? Is it a compliment to a father to say, "He never said no to his children?" Of course not. So if we, evil as we are, know it is at times best for our children *not* to give them what they want, what they are so sure they *need,* how much more does our heavenly Father know what's best for us? "Know then in your heart that as a man disciplines his son, so the LORD your God disciplines you" (Deuteronomy 8:5).

We hear a great deal today about the church meeting our needs. We have small groups for every type of recovery. We tailor worship to the desires of different age groups. We buy books and attend seminars to solve our every problem. None of these are bad in themselves, but they can easily lead us into temptation. We are tempted to think that God is there to meet our every need, to turn all our stones to bread. Instead, he may throw rocks along our path simply to remind us that we need one thing only. We do not need self-esteem, success, money, friendship, happy families nor exciting churches; but God himself is our one true need.

Jesus knew what it was like to be hungry, so he fed the hungry. He would not turn stones to bread for himself, but he would multiply loaves and fish for others. He feeds us too. More than that, he teaches us how to be hungry: hunger for God, not for food. God alone can satisfy.

What Doesn't Satisfy

The lesson of the temptation and the miraculous feedings is the same: Jesus alone satisfies. The disciples saw Jesus feed the five thousand, then the four thousand, but they didn't understand the lesson. They still didn't know how to be hungry.

Immediately after the feeding of the four thousand, Jesus and the disciples get into a boat. The disciples forgot to bring bread for the journey, except for one loaf. This is right after the Pharisees had demanded a sign from Jesus.

Jesus warns the disciples, "Beware of the yeast of the Pharisees and Herod."

"Oh, no!" the disciples think. "He knows we forgot the bread. That's why he's talking about yeast."

With their own eyes, the disciples had seen what Jesus could do with a loaf of bread: he could feed a multitude. Now they worry that they might not have enough bread. How stupid could they be? Jesus reminds them of the miracles of the loaves and asks, "Do you still not understand?" (Mark 8:21).

No answer comes.

It's amazing, but they didn't understand.

Do we?

Sure we do. We know Jesus was talking about the teaching of the Pharisees and Herod. He was warning the disciples not to think like them. The Pharisees could see the mighty hand of Jesus in the feeding of the four thousand and still demand a sign. No matter what Jesus did, they were never satisfied. The yeast or bread of the Pharisees was this unbelief. The bread of unbelief can never fill disciples like the bread of Jesus.

Is the bread of the Pharisees still with us today? I'm afraid it is. Some disciples still demand signs from Jesus in spite of how he has fed us in the past. "Yes, Lord," we say, "I know you've taken care of me in the past. I've never been hungry. You've healed me when I'm sick. You've given me family and friends to cheer me. You've filled my every need."

"But what have you done for me lately?"

Isn't this the attitude of the Pharisees who demand a sign? Are we guilty of the same? If you say no, then tell me: If you trust Jesus to provide for you, why do you buy all those things you see on TV?

"That's going too far," you say. "There's nothing wrong with buying toothpaste or deodorant or tennis shoes. We need those things."

We may. The question is not, "Did you buy the products?" but "Did you buy the advertising?" Do you deep down believe that this product, this technique, this "new and improved" thing will bring you a bit more happiness? Do you in any way think it really satisfies? Does it actually make life better?

If so, we (like the Pharisees) are looking for satisfaction in the wrong places. Like them, we are not content with Jesus. We want more.

What Really Satisfies

You cannot have the world and have God too. You cannot rely on physical bread and expect the bread that really satisfies. This is the lesson Jesus learned in the wilderness. There is only one thing that satisfies. One kind of bread brings life: the bread of God. The Word of God.

We Christians, like the disciples, sometimes do not understand. We still live as if the things of this world can make us happy. We still trust our bank accounts instead of the One who turns one loaf into many. One lesson of the feeding miracles: Jesus can give us all the food we need. The greatest lesson: Jesus alone can give us the food that truly satisfies..

In the Gospel of John, after he feeds the five thousand, Jesus clearly states the lesson of the miracle:

Then Jesus declared, "I am the bread of life. He who comes to me will never go hungry, and he who believes in me will never be thirsty" (John 6:35).

Jesus feeds not just with bread, but with himself. He satisfies more than physical hunger.

Are you hungry? I know you are. We all have hungers. Deep, true hungers. We hunger for food, for friendship, for understanding, for meaning, for belonging.

To be human is to hunger. Jesus knows what it's like to be hungry, so he feeds the hungry. He fills all hungers.

Are we satisfied with Jesus? Or do we hunger for all the other things that promise to satisfy? They promise, but can't deliver. Jesus feeds and we never go hungry.

We are disciples. We follow Jesus. Of course we are satisfied with him. How do we express that satisfaction? We begin by talking back to our televisions. When we see those ads for products that claim to satisfy, we laugh and say, "Who do you think you're fooling? Buying you will make me no happier. Only One satisfies."

What else do we do? We intentionally refuse to buy. Why? Because those things are bad? No, because we need to learn the lesson Jesus learned in the wilderness. There was nothing evil about the bread Jesus wanted. He still didn't change the stones. Why? Because he remembered what really satisfies. If we choose to deprive ourselves of certain things, we too will be reminded of what satisfies. We will discover our true hunger. We want Jesus, not some new thing.

We talk back to TV. We say no to certain purchases. We must do more. We must pass true values on to our children. We must learn and then teach by our lives what is of true value. We are hungry. Nothing on earth satisfies. Only the Word of God.

The crowd is in a deserted place. There's nowhere they can go to get bread. One alone can feed them. He does. He gives them more than they can eat.

Jesus knows what it is like to be hungry. He teaches us how to be hungry.

Jesus really satisfies.

CHAPTER TEN

NO TIME FOR HUMOR

Luke 8:40-42, 49-56

"They laughed at him" Luke 8:53.

Funny things happen in church. Things that wouldn't provoke a chuckle elsewhere cause loud laughter in church. Children are sometimes especially funny because they haven't learned that church is a place of serious business.

It was the middle of the sermon in a church I was visiting. The preacher was going on about some Bible doctrine; I don't remember what. My memory of his sermon is fuzzy because he had some serious competition. A two-year-old boy who sat near me drowned out the preacher with his own talking. "Quiet!" his father whispered time after time. It did no good. The boy continued to talk.

Finally the exasperated father stood up, tucked his son under his arm, and headed toward the back of the church. As he reached the back door, his son shouted in a loud voice, "Y'all pray for me!"

I'm sure I'm not the only one who forgot the rest of the sermon.

On another occasion I was passing the collection plate throughout the congregation. As I got near the back pew, the nearly full plate was passed from hand to hand down the row. A boy who'd been playing under the pew chose that precise moment to pop up. His head hit the bottom of the collection plate, coins and bills flew through the air, and the sound of his childish crying mingled with that of stifled adult laughter.

It happens in weddings too. When my sister-in-law Sandy got married, everyone looked elegant. The groom and groomsmen were in tuxedos, the bridesmaids in their beautiful dresses. Sandy was particularly lovely. Standing there with the preacher, they made a picture-perfect Norman Rockwell portrait of nuptial bliss. With one exception. The young ring bearer spent the entire ceremony twirling the satin ring pillow round and round his head.

We could multiply such scenes indefinitely. Funny things happen in church — at worship, in weddings, even at times of fellowship. There is one time at church that is never funny.

There's nothing funny about a funeral.

Nothing Funny

It was the greatest day of my life.

I came home from work that day, and my wife, Deb, met me at the door. She'd been to the doctor that day and I was eager to get the news. She threw her arms around me and said, "You're going to be a daddy."

I could do nothing but smile.

Deb and I had waited for years to have children. We'd waited so long that some of our friends and family thought we were kidding when we told them we were expecting. Now it was going to happen. The next few weeks I spent each day in a state somewhere between anticipation and terror. We dreamed and planned for the child that was coming. Finding an old baby bed at a garage sale, we lovingly refinished it and placed it in the nursery. We talked of how long Deb would work. We agreed on a boy's name, but had trouble deciding what to name a girl. Each night I went to bed wondering what kind of father I would be.

There was nothing funny about the worst day of my life.

Deb was going for a routine check-up. We discussed whether I should go with her, but decided there was no need.

I was sitting at home when the phone rang. I couldn't make out the words because Deb was crying so. She gave the phone to the doctor who gave the news. Miscarriage. Our baby was dead.

The next few hours were a blur of second opinions, procedures, doctor's offices and the hospital. For Deb's sake (and mine), I had to be strong. I kept telling myself, "This isn't happening." But it was.

It was months before Deb slept without waking up in tears in the middle of the night. I cried less often, at least on the outside, but even today, tears still come. Not a day goes by without my thinking of my unborn child.

Many tried to comfort us in our grief. Some were more successful than others. The most comfort came from those who said, "I don't have any idea what you're going through, but we want you to know that we love you." The worst comforters were those who acted as if it were no big deal. "It's not as if you lost a real child," they seemed to say. In other words, "Face reality and get over it."

Easier said than done.

They Laughed

There's nothing funny about the death of a child. I can't imagine anything more painful. When the innocent are taken from us, we not only grieve, but we are tempted to doubt the justice of the universe. "Why not me?" we cry, "Why didn't God take me instead of my beautiful little girl?"

The pain is worse if she was an only child. Just ask Jairus. A righteous man, a ruler of the synagogue, yet illness strikes his only child, his beloved twelve-year old daughter.

Jairus is distraught. Beside himself with worry. His only hope is the young teacher from Nazareth. Yet he's not sure Jesus will help him, for Jairus and the other synagogue rulers had run Jesus out of their synagogues for healing on the Sabbath. Now it was different. Now it's his daughter who is at death's door. Jairus doesn't care about Jesus' orthodoxy. He doesn't care if he heals his girl today or on the Sabbath. He just wants his little girl well again.

So he goes to Jesus, falls at his feet and begs him to come heal her. Jesus holds no grudges. He agrees to come. Hope swells within Jairus. The Rabbi will heal her. All would be well.

Suddenly, a servant blocks their path. With tears running down his face he says, "Your daughter is dead; don't trouble the teacher any longer." The blow Jairus feared had fallen. His little girl was gone. All hope was gone.

"Why bother the teacher anymore?" the servant says. In other words, "Accept what's happened and get over it. Don't harbor false hopes." Jairus is ready to accept this advice. He's ready to begin the grieving process by resigning himself to the awful truth. His little girl is gone. He'll see her no more.

But Jesus won't let that happen. He completely ignores the news that the girl is dead. Instead he tells Jairus, "Don't be afraid; just believe" (Mark 5:36). What is Jesus doing? Is he encouraging this poor man to ignore reality and live in a fool's paradise? Is he saying it is healthy to live in denial? No. Jesus points Jairus to a deeper reality. Things are not what they seem. Do not be afraid of what seems real. Only believe.

So Jesus insists on coming to his house anyway. A great crowd has gathered to mourn. He enters the house and they all — Jesus, Peter, James, John, the girl's parents, and the crowd — stand around her bed. All but Jesus cry, the parents in particular pouring out their grief. Then Jesus says, "She is not dead but asleep."

And they laughed.

What kind of inappropriate joke was this? They all knew she was dead. It was cruel and foolish to suggest otherwise. What would we think of a person who interrupts a funeral by going to the casket, and saying, "I saw her breathing. She's not dead, just asleep"? We'd think it the sickest of jokes. We'd laugh, not out of amusement, but out of ridicule. What was Jesus thinking?

He was thinking that he saw something the others did not see. They saw a dead girl. They saw death as final. Jesus saw a deeper truth.

He sends the crowd from the room. He takes the dead girl by the hand and says gently, "Little girl, get up." She does. He presents her to her astonished parents. So amazed are they that Jesus has to remind them what their little girl needs. "Give her something to eat," he says with a smile.

An astounding, unbelievable miracle. Yet it is not the miracle that surprises us today. We know this story. We know Jesus did miracles. What surprises us is the laughter. How could they have laughed? Didn't they know the power of God? Hadn't the disciples seen the miracles of Jesus? What little faith they had.

Are we any better? Don't we have problems that seem beyond the reach of immediate solution? We all have private demons, habitual sins that we cannot seem to shake. What if Jesus said, "You have no struggles"? Would we believe him or would we laugh?

We all have friends and family who wrestle with insurmountable problems: marital difficulties, alcoholism, child abuse, financial worries, depression, and despair. Do we really believe Jesus can solve our problems or do we laugh at such a suggestion?

The truth is Jesus has not promised to immediately solve all our problems. He didn't promise to raise this girl from the dead. But he did. He had the grace and he had the power. Not even their laughter prevented him.

At times our problems seem as insurmountable as death itself. But Jesus has the power to say, "What problem?" just as he had the love to say, "She merely sleeps." We must never despair of that power and that love. He has promised to work everything for our good. When we hear that promise, we must believe. When we hear that promise, there is one thing we must not do.

We dare not laugh. For he holds life in his hand, and he can do the impossible.

Other Funerals

Not only can he do the impossible, he does. Again.

Jesus and his disciples encounter a funeral on their way into the village of Nain. Another child dead. A young man. We don't know his age, but we do know he too was an only child. The only child of a widow.

That made his death doubly painful. His mother faced grief and poverty. In the ancient world, a woman rarely worked outside the home. Her husband supported her. If her husband died, her sons took care of her. This woman had lost more than a beloved son; she had lost all means of financially making a living.

Jesus comes and sees the woman. His heart goes out to her and he says, "Don't cry." Then he does the unthinkable.

He interrupts the funeral.

One can imagine what those in the funeral procession thought.

"What does he think he's doing?"

"How embarrassing!"

"Can't he leave this poor widow alone?"

But he stops the pallbearers in their tracks. Placing

his hands on the coffin, he says, "Young man, I say to you, get up!" (Luke 7:14).

He does. He sits up and begins to talk. Jesus helps him out of his coffin and gives him back to his mother.

Jesus had fun at funerals. I don't mean he was unfeeling. He wept at the tomb of Lazarus. But like a child in church, he didn't know funerals were serious business. Or rather, he knew something others could only laugh at. He knew death was not the end.

In the past year I attended the funerals of two similar men. Both were faithful Christians. Both were successful businessmen.

The men were similar, but their funerals were quite different. At one, lawyers, professors, doctors, and family members all took turns recounting the accomplishments of the deceased. They justly praised him as a remarkable family man, scholar, and entrepreneur. Oh, they also briefly mentioned his ties to the church.

The other funeral had a different focus. The man was no less successful than the first, but those who spoke talked not of his accomplishments but of his faith. They also reminded us of what was truly important about this man: he will live again in the resurrection.

I think Jesus would have had more fun at the second funeral. I did. Not shallow humor or fun, but that deep conviction about and joy over what is important and real and final.

Laughing at Death

Jesus said Jairus' daughter was only asleep. "They laughed at him, knowing that she was dead" (Luke 8:53). They laugh at Jesus because they know he's wrong.

He has the last laugh. He told the honest truth. Death is not final. It is only sleep.

The early Christians learned this lesson from Jesus. They too call death sleep.

Paul tells the Corinthians that if death is the end, then everything, even our faith, is useless. We are even worse off than the Old Testament characters who knew nothing of life after death. It is better to ask "Who knows?" about death, than to claim to know and find you are deceived.

But we are not deceived. Our faith is not mere wishful thinking.

But Christ has indeed been raised from the dead, the firstfruits of those who have fallen asleep (I Corinthians 15:20).

Christ is risen! He lives! This is the heart of the Christian faith. This is what we celebrate each Sunday. This we believe. Do you believe? Do you know that Jesus lives, that he triumphed over death? I think any Christian would say, "Yes." We may have our doubts, but in our heart of hearts we know he is alive.

And we know if he is alive, then death is not final. It is only sleep. And one day Jesus will return and bring the sleepers with him.

Brothers, we do not want you to be ignorant about those who fall asleep, or to grieve like the rest of men, who have no hope. We believe that Jesus died and rose again and so we believe that God will bring with Jesus those who have fallen asleep in him (I Thessalonians 4:13-14).

Jesus teaches us how to laugh at funerals. Not that we literally laugh. That would be cruel to those who grieve. We do laugh inwardly at death itself. We laugh because we know the day is coming when death itself will die (Revelation 20:14). We laugh because our loved ones are not dead. They only sleep. We laugh not because we have gotten over our losses. We may never get over them in this life. We laugh because our loved ones will get over death.

I'll never be able to laugh at the death of my child. Not in this life. But I know the day is coming when my little girl or little boy will hear the words of Jesus: "My child, get up!"

Then I will laugh.

CHAPTER ELEVEN

SET FREE!

John 11:1-44

"Unbind him, and let him go" John 11:44 (NRSV).

In eighteen years of teaching in high school and college, I've heard many graduation speeches. They all went something like this:

"Now young people, I want you to know today that your whole life lies in front of you. Your opportunities are unlimited. There is nothing you can't accomplish if you have determination. Nothing can limit you or slow you down unless you let it."

There are two problems with such graduation speeches. They're always too long (I gave a much condensed summary), and they're just not true. It's a lie that there are no limitations in life. The older one lives, the more one sees limits.

We are limited by our talents. No one is good at everything. There are things we cannot do no matter how hard we try. I'll never be a center in the NBA no matter how hard I try or how positive my attitude. Why? I'm too short, too slow, too small, and too old. Oh yeah, and I can't hit a jump shot.

We are limited by our timing. If you're not in the right place at the right time, you won't succeed. I'm sure that I am the best qualified person for many exciting and prestigious jobs. Unfortunately, they are not open at the moment.

We are limited by our responsibilities to those around us. To family. Think what we could accomplish if we were not tied down to wife, husband, kids, house, and dog. Our churches limit our opportunities. We can't focus on our own spiritual needs because we have to care for others.

To be human is to be limited. These limits are not all bad, unless we think we have the right to be all we can be at the expense of others.

The Ultimate Limit

An older man is talking with an ambitious high school graduate.

"What are your plans now?"

"I plan to go to college and major in business."

"Then what?"

"Well, after I graduate, I'll go on and get an M.B.A."

"Then what?"

"Then I'll start my own business.

"Then what?"

"I guess I'll get married and have kids, the whole family thing."

"Then what?'

"Who knows? After I make a lot of money I may even go into politics or something."

"Then what?"

"Well, when the kids leave home, I can retire and take it easy."

"Then what?"

"I guess I'll get old."

"Then what?"

"Eventually, I'll die."

"Then what?"

Death is the ultimate limit. It laughs at all our pretensions of unlimited potential. No matter what we accomplish in life, death comes. The question is what comes next?

Death certainly looks final. We hope for life beyond the grave, but that very hope makes us doubt. Perhaps our quest for the afterlife is just wishful thinking. "We shouldn't think this way," we tell ourselves. "Our faith should be stronger." Yet the doubts still come.

It is strange that we find one of the most eloquent expressions of that doubt where we least expect it: in the Bible itself.

I also thought, "As for men, God tests them so that they may see that they are like the animals. Man's fate is like that of the animals; the same fate awaits them both: As one dies, so dies the other. All have the same breath; man has no advantage over the animal. Everything is meaningless. All go to the same place; all come from dust, and to dust all return. Who knows if the spirit of man rises upward and if the spirit of the animal goes down into the earth?" (Ecclesiastes 3:18-21).

What's this doing in the Bible? Aren't we to fight our doubts? Aren't they signs of unbelief?

Maybe. But they are human. The Bible never flinches from the reality of human feeling. The writer of Ecclesiastes looks death in the face and he doesn't blink. The body goes into the grave and it looks like it's all over. It looks no different to bury a human than a dog. Both turn to dust.

To appreciate these verses we need to understand the view of the afterlife in the Old Testament. As far as we know, God gave Israel no clear word on life after death. They were left to their own experience and speculation. Their experience said death was final. One places the body in the tomb. It stays there. The dead do not return. Death is the end, the great leveler of life. All human accomplishment crumbles into insignificance because of this one fact: all die.

Their speculation and hope said otherwise. Perhaps

there is some life beyond *sheol*, the Hebrew word for grave, but we know little about it. To the Hebrews, *sheol* was a shadowy existence, not as substantial as this life. They thought that perhaps God's covenant stretched even beyond death. There may be a place where the faithful continue to serve their God. But who knows? Who can be sure?

Unsure of any real afterlife, the Hebrews and other ancient peoples tried to find a measure of immortality in their children and their reputations. Many moderns try the same. We expect our children to carry on our name after us, to keep our memory alive. But how many of us know our great-grandmothers' maiden names? In a generation or two, our families will forget us. Many try to gain immortality from monuments: a building, a statue, a book, or a tombstone. None last. A few months ago I visited the ruins of St. Kevin's monastery in Ireland, a burial place of Christians for centuries. Hundreds of tombstones dot the landscape; most are worn smooth. The earliest date I could read was 1728. If we count on the immortality of remembrance, it is a brief one. In a few years our names will be forgotten.

Yet in spite of the Hebrews' ignorance of the afterlife, they were still faithful to their God. This is the most amazing aspect of Old Testament faith. With no fear of eternal punishment or hope of eternal reward, they continued to serve and obey God. Knowing only of this life, they chose to honor the covenant their fathers made with the Lord.

The Resurrection and the Life

This was the world of the disciples, a world where few were sure there was life after death. But Jesus came proclaiming the resurrection, convincing many they would rise again at the last day.

One day he convinced them of much more than that.

Jesus is teaching when he receives word that Lazarus is sick. Instead of rushing to his side, Jesus delays his journey for two days. When he decides to go to Lazarus, he confuses his disciples (as he confused the family of Jairus) by saying, "Lazarus has fallen asleep." "Then he'll get better," the disciples reply. He then tells them plainly, "Lazarus is dead."

As they approach Bethany, Martha greets Jesus with these words, "Lord, if you had been here, my brother would not have died."

Jesus answers, "Your brother will rise again."

"I know he will rise again in the resurrection at the last day," says Martha.

This is a great confession of faith. In spite of the lack of Old Testament teaching on the afterlife, Martha is sure her brother will live again. She is sure because of Jesus. Her confession is great, but not great enough.

Jesus says to her, "I am the resurrection and the life. He who believes in me will live, even though he dies; and whoever lives and believes in me will never die" (John 11:25-26).

It's an amazing idea that someday we will rise from the dead. As Christians we believe it. Like Martha, we know it. But Jesus does more than promise a resurrection someday. He is the resurrection. Where Jesus is, there can be no death.

We know that from the rest of the story. Jesus sees the pain of Mary and Martha. He shares that pain. He weeps with them. Some standing there do not believe he really cares. "Could not he who opened the eyes of the blind man have kept this man from dying?" they ask (John 11:37).

Jesus shows his compassion in a way they could not imagine. He goes to the tomb and says, "Roll away the stone." Then, after praying, he commands, "Lazarus, come out!"

And Lazarus comes. Alive.

To Lazarus the answer to "Then what?" was simple. After death, he saw Jesus. The answer is the same for us. After death, resurrection.

Jesus raises Lazarus from the dead as a preview of his own resurrection. I believe with my whole heart that Jesus was raised from the dead. Yet strangely I find it easier to believe in the resurrection of Christ than in my own resurrection. Death seems so much like the end. We don't know what comes beyond. If only someone we trust could return to tell us what it will be like.

One has! His name is Lazarus. Another has. His name is Jesus. His resurrection is not just some old historic fact. His resurrection is our resurrection. He's the firstfruits, Paul says, the preview of what will happen to us all. If we believe Jesus was raised from the dead, then we can be sure our mothers, fathers, wives, husbands, and children will be raised. We know the ultimate end of our own death: resurrection, new life.

What keeps us from believing? Our distrust of wishful thinking? We may want so much to believe that death is not the end, that our own desire to believe makes us doubt. We know that wishing for something doesn't make it true. Neither does it make it false. If our heart's desire is for life after death, we may get what we want. More than "may," we will, if we shift our focus from our desires to what happened two thousand years ago on a hillside in Judea. The tomb was empty. Lazarus was alive. He ate and drank and spoke. A few days later another tomb would be empty. Resurrection himself came back to life.

What keeps us from believing? Our scientific age? We know that bodies decay; they turn to dust; they are scattered to the four winds. We know people don't come back from the grave. Science proves it. We also know human beings do not walk on water, still storms by their words, or turn one boy's lunch into enough to feed five thousand. But one did. The same God who gave him that power is the God who raised him from the dead. He's the same God who will raise us.

What keeps us from believing? Perhaps more than anything it's our own view of death. Too many funerals, too many graves convince us that death is the end. It is not. Christ is risen. With his resurrection he changed the face of death forever. Death lives on borrowed time. The day will come when death itself will die (Revelation 20:14), when we will live forever with our risen Lord.

> When the perishable has been clothed with the imperishable, and the mortal with immortality, then the saying that is written will come true: "Death has been swallowed up in victory."
> "Where, O death, is your victory?
> Where, O death, is your sting?"
> The sting of death is sin, and the power of sin is the law. But thanks be to God! He gives us the victory through our Lord Jesus Christ (I Corinthians 15:54-57).

Life Without Limits

We believe that the day of resurrection will come. We believe more than that. We believe Jesus when he said he is the resurrection and the life.

What difference does that make in our lives now? The difference is summed up in the words Jesus spoke after he raised Lazarus. Lazarus came from the tomb still bound by his grave clothes. Jesus said, "Unbind him, and let him go."

We live our lives bound, limited, tied up like Lazarus. We are not yet dead, but the fear of death ties our hands and limits all we do. Jesus changes all that. Now he sets us free from death. He unbinds that fear that shrouds our hearts.

Since the children have flesh and blood, he too shared in their humanity so that by his death he might destroy him who holds the power of death — that is, the devil — and free those who all their lives were held in slavery by their fear of death. (Hebrews 2:14-15).

To be human is to be limited, but we need not fear the greatest limit of all. For those outside of Christ, death puts an end to all their accomplishments, hopes, and dreams. Not so for us who know Jesus as the resurrection and the life.

Some criticize Christians for being too otherworldly. They say we care little about the injustices of this life because we believe in pie in the sky by and by when we die. Nothing could be further from biblical truth. The Bible teaches that our faith in the resurrection makes life more significant, not less. For Old Testament saints, death almost made life worthless; if it all ends at death, then what use is anything we do? For New Testament saints, the promise of eternal life begins now. Because we will live anew forever, we believe this life is real, that it is a test, a preparation for the life to come.

Paul uses the truth of Jesus' resurrection and the assurance of our own to motivate us to faithfulness and work in this life:

Therefore, my dear brothers, stand firm. Let nothing move you. Always give yourselves fully to the work of the Lord, because you know that your labor in the Lord is not in vain (1 Corinthians 15:58).

"Labor is vanity," says Ecclesiastes, because the writer could not see beyond his death. "Your labor is not in vain," says Paul, because he knew the end of death itself. Each day we live we celebrate the resurrection of Jesus. Each day we anticipate a reunion with our loved ones.

Each day we work for our Lord, knowing that someday we will stand before him in a new body. He rose. So will we.

Our task is to stand fast, to not be moved. Our doubts will assail us. Stand fast. Our friends will scoff. Stand fast. We will grow tired. Stand fast. Our work will not go unrewarded.

When Jesus raised Lazarus, he raised us too. He showed that he will raise us at the last day. He showed that he has the power to raise us now. He is resurrection. The life we live in him is new life, resurrection life. He is the life. We believe in him and we will never die. Like Lazarus, we will only sleep. Like Lazarus, we hear his voice. Like Lazarus, we feel his hands free us from all that binds.

Even death.

CHAPTER TWELVE

THE GREATEST
MIRACLE OF ALL

Matthew 27:31-54

"Then they led him away to crucify him" Matthew 27:31.

What was the greatest miracle Jesus performed?

Healing the man born blind? Here was a miracle no one could dispute or explain away. The man wasn't hysterically blind; he didn't just think he was blind; he was blind from birth. Jesus puts mud on his eyes, tells him to wash, and the man washes away not only mud but his blindness. The man exclaims: "Nobody has ever heard of opening the eyes of a man born blind" (John 9:32). A miracle. An unheard of miracle. The greatest miracle of all?

What about the miracle of the bread and the fish? Surely that was the greatest of all. And Jesus doesn't do it once, but twice. He feeds 5000 with five loaves and two fish. A few days later, he feeds 4000 with seven loaves and a few small fish. In each case, after they are full he ends up with more bread than he started with. Now that is a miracle! Unlike the healings, this wonder does not depend on the people's faith, but solely on the power and generosity of Jesus. These must be the greatest miracles.

But the greatest enemy of all is death. The greatest miracle must be resurrection. Jesus runs into a funeral as he enters the town of Nain. A widow's only son is being buried. Jesus raises him from the dead (Luke 7:11-17). A ruler of the synagogue asks Jesus to come and heal his sick daughter, an only child. Before Jesus gets to his house, the message comes, "Don't bother the teacher. Your daughter is dead." Jesus promises to heal her anyway. He shocks her parents by raising her from the dead. Can any miracle rival resurrection?

Yes. There is one that is greater. The miracle of the cross. Here one who was blameless, sinless, perfect, dies for the world. He dies for the very ones who crucify him. He dies for me. For you. Can there be a greater miracle than this miracle of love?

But isn't that stretching the idea of miracle a bit? The crucifixion is amazing, no doubt of that, but is it a miracle?

There was one who thought so. One who was there, who saw Jesus crucified. One who crucified him. Let us go to Calvary and see this miracle through his eyes.

Another Day, Another Drachma

He was back home in Italy, by the sea. The tang of the salt air filled his lungs as a smile spread over his face. "Surely this is paradise," he thought.

Suddenly the sea faded, replaced by the homely face of one of his men.

"Wake up, Sir. The governor wants to see you."

For a moment he wasn't sure where he was. Then it hit him. The heat, the smell. He wasn't back home by the sea; he was in the stinking province of Palestine. Oh well, no one ever told him that soldiering would be easy. He's been in enough stink-holes in his long career to have learned that. It was time to earn his pay. Another day, another drachma.

Putting on his uniform, he rushed to the governor's palace. Pilate had a job for him all right, an execution, in fact, three. He'd been in charge of countless crucifixions before. It wasn't his favorite job, but it was routine.

Two of the prisoners were like all the ones before them. They'd repeatedly broken the Roman peace, robbing their fellow Jews in the guise of freedom fighters. Hah! As if anyone in this accursed country could lead a successful rebellion. The third prisoner was different. He was being put to death because of some disagreements he had with the Jewish leaders over their laws. The Jews had convinced Pilate that he was politically dangerous, so he ordered him crucified. Word was that this man Jesus had not even tried to defend himself at his trial. "What a loser," thought the centurion.

Until he saw him. There was something in his eyes and in the way he walked. This Jesus didn't have the look of a prisoner. But that would change. Pilate had ordered him flogged. No one could stand a flogging and still keep his dignity.

"Strip him and beat him," the centurion ordered. As the flogging began, he was distracted by preparations for the crucifixion. "Are the crosses ready?" he asked the private. "Corporal, make sure you have enough men for crowd control." As he gave his orders, something nagged at the back of his mind. It was the flogging. Something wasn't quite right.

Then it hit him. The silence. This Jew Jesus was taking his beating in silence. Not a word escaped his lips. In all his years he'd never witnessed anything like it. Maybe there was some truth to those rumors that Jesus possessed some special power.

His thoughts were interrupted by another soldier calling him away for some last minute preparations. When he returned, he found his troops having fun at the expense of the prisoner. They'd heard that his crime was claiming to be King of the Jews, so they put a kingly robe on him, gave him a crown of thorns, and beat him on the head with his own wooden "scepter." While some spat at him, others kneeled before him. "Look at me, guys," one said, "I'm joining with this Jewish king."

His first impulse was to break things up. Flogging and crucifixion were cruel enough without adding insult to injury. What stopped him in his tracks was the face of this Jesus. The insults fazed him not in the least. He sat there quietly as if nothing was happening. The centurion was so shocked, by the time he recovered, the soldiers were through with their fun.

They forced Jesus and the other prisoners to carry their crosses to Skull Hill outside the city. Jesus fell repeatedly, until finally the centurion ran out of patience and grabbed someone from the crowd to carry his cross. As the procession wound through the city, the crowds jeered the prisoners, saving their most hateful threats for Jesus.

When they got to the Skull, the centurion was busy. He made sure the prisoners were nailed tight to their crosses and that they were raised in the proper manner. He had their charges nailed over them, including Jesus' crime: "King of the Jews." He let the soldiers gamble for the prisoners' clothes. Then, as he had done so many times before, he settled down to wait for them to die.

Something was different about this time. It all had to do with this prisoner Jesus. Something about his eyes. In pain, they still reflected his care for others. The crowd jeered at him. Even his fellow prisoners joined in. It didn't bother him. Indeed, his calmness caused one of the thieves to change his mind. This Jesus just didn't die like all the others.

Then the centurion heard the last words he ever expected to hear from one on a cross: "Father, forgive them, they do not know what they are doing." He'd been cursed so many times from so many crosses, that he paid no attention to it anymore. But he'd never been blessed, never forgiven. This Jesus was no ordinary man.

For hours the centurion stood there and watched him, transfixed by the way this Jesus died. Then he heard him cry in a loud voice. He couldn't understand the words, but he knew he was crying to his God.

Then Jesus died.

At that moment the centurion was startled. A strange darkness had covered the land for hours. Now the ground began to shake. He couldn't keep his footing. His men were terrified.

This hardened soldier, not prone to emotional outbursts, could not believe what he had witnessed. "Surely this was no ordinary man," he thought. "Surely he was innocent." "Surely, he was the Son of God."

Great Miracles

Here stands a pagan. An unbeliever. A hard-headed soldier not given to foolishness. He knew little of Jesus. He only knew how he died. But he is convinced. This Jesus is from God. It's not clear exactly what he confessed. According to Luke, he proclaimed Christ "righteous" or "innocent." Mark and Matthew say he called him "the Son of God," or, as some translations say, "a son of God." Whatever the depth of his confession, the amazing thing is that he had faith at all. He didn't see Jesus teaching the crowds. He didn't see him confound the religious teachers. He never saw him heal the sick or raise the dead. He wasn't at the empty tomb. He only saw him on the cross. That was enough.

What does it take for us to follow Jesus, to confess him each day as the Son of God? Does it take teaching that touches our hearts? Blessings? Miracles? Or like this centurion can we see him at his greatest defeat, at the lowest point of his life, and still see there the Holy Son of God? We see him at the cross. He bids us to take our own and follow.

Is the crucifixion a miracle? Certainly miracles surround it: darkness, earthquake, even dead brought back to life (Matthew 27:52-53). When Jesus dies, another miracle takes place that we are prone to overlook: "At that moment the curtain of the temple was torn in two from top to bottom" (Matthew 27:51).

127

It's one of those small phrases that gets lost in the accounts of the crucifixion. We tend to read over it quickly and forget it, or if it does catch our attention, we think, "What's that doing there?" It seems like an extraneous detail to the story. Jesus has just died for the sins of the world; why talk about a curtain being torn?

There is something in these few words that strikes at the heart of what it means to be a Christian. We all know the significance of the tearing of the temple curtain or veil. This was the thick curtain that divided the Holy Place from the Most Holy Place. The Presence of God inhabited the Most Holy Place in some special way. It was so holy, that only the high priest could enter, then only once a year on the Day of Atonement, and only with sacrificial blood for his own sins.

The symbolism of the torn curtain is clear: through Jesus' death, the path to God is made open to everyone. All may approach his holy throne through the blood of Jesus. We no longer need a human priest to stand between us and God. Christ alone is our mediator and we all are priests. God himself will now hear our requests through Jesus Christ.

But the part of the verse we may miss is that the curtain is torn *from top to bottom*. In other words, it was no human act that opened the way to God. It was no superhuman effort on our part that scaled the heights to bring God down to us. No! It was God himself and God alone in the person of his Son who opens the door for us.

This is not just a story about how a curtain was torn, it is a metaphor for the whole of the Christian life. Too many times we live as if the depth of our relationship to God was all up to us. If only we could sin less and pray more. If only we had the right technique, the right steps. If only we could find the right book that would unlock the secret of spirituality.

It doesn't work that way. Christian faith and spirituality don't come from the bottom up. They come from the top down. God does them for us. He opens the way. Yes, we must walk through the curtain, but even there we have someone to follow. We follow in the steps of One whose love and obedience and very blood opened the curtain for us. He ripped it open, from top to bottom.

The Greatest Miracle

We know miracles accompanied the crucifixion, but is Jesus' death on the cross itself a miracle? It's never actually called one in the Bible, but it fits the words the Bible uses to describe miracles.

What words are used for the miracles of Jesus in the Bible? At Pentecost, Peter calls Jesus, "a man attested to you by God with deeds of power, wonders, and signs . . ." (Acts 2:22, NRSV). Jesus performed deeds of power. Was the crucifixion an act of power? Yes, the most powerful act in history. This act overcomes the power of sin and Satan. This act changes the whole course of history. This act transforms all humanity. There has never been a greater display of power. By embracing the powerlessness of the cross, Jesus unleashes a tidal force of love that sweeps all away before it. We sing, "There's power in the blood." Indeed there is. No greater power exists. No greater miracle.

Jesus' death on the cross is a deed of power. It is also a wonder. A wonder is something that astonishes and surprises. Something uncanny, almost terrifying.

Does the cross surprise? Jesus' death should not have been a surprise to his disciples. More than once he'd told them plainly that he must go to Jerusalem, suffer at the hands of the chief priests, and be crucified. They should have known. They didn't. They were completely caught off guard by his arrest and execution.

Jesus' death is no surprise to us. It's the center of our faith. He died for me, for you. Countless sermons have been preached, countless books written on his death. Yet the story still surprises. It catches us off guard when we consider not just that he died for us, but how he died for us. What he says and what he doesn't say, what he does and what he doesn't do, all amaze us with the depth of his obedience and his love.

He was alone. All fled and deserted him. Even the Father forsook him. Most who saw the crucifixion were his enemies: the crowd who jeered him, the soldiers who crucified him, even his fellow prisoners who died with him. He surprised them too. The bitter hatred of the crowd could not keep him from his destiny. One thief turns to him in repentance. A hardened centurion confesses faith.

Here is the greatest wonder of all: not how he died, but why he died. He died for me, for you. Such love shocks us. We gaze open-mouthed at this one on the cross. He is a wonder. The greatest wonder of them all. The greatest miracle.

Power. Wonder. Miracles are also signs. A sign points to something beyond itself. The miracles of Jesus point to a deeper reality. They point to God. The cross is a sign-post of the love of God. In the cross we clearly see the God of love. He loved us so much he sent his Son to die for us. We did not, we do not deserve such love. Still he loves, for his love is free. Free to us. Costly to him. In the cross we see a sign of that awful cost. Here the Son of God, God himself, pays the ultimate price of love.

We are all familiar with signs of love. We see them daily. A guy gives a girl his class ring. A little girl writes her mother a sweet note. A grandfather passes on a cherished book to his grandson. We treasure the ring, the note, the book, not because they are valuable in themselves, but because they are signs of love.

In our society the cross has lost much of its power as a sign. Perhaps we see it too often. We see it not just on churches, but as jewelry around the necks of rock stars who by their actions blaspheme the One who died on it. We even see the Klan burning it in yards as a sign of hatred and racism. To many the cross has lost its power to point to God.

Not for us. We are those who cherish the old rugged cross. We cherish it not as an empty sign, but as the greatest power and wonder of all. We cherish it not just as a sign of Jesus' love but as a sign of our relationship to him. Jesus bids us share the greatest miracle of all, the miracle of the crucifixion. "Take up your cross daily and follow me." In the words of the hymn, "Go to Dark Gethsemane," by James Montgomery:

> *Calv'ry's mournful mountain climb;*
> *There, adoring at His feet*
> *Mark that miracle of time,*
> *God's own sacrifice complete:*
> *"It is finished!" hear him cry;*
> *Learn of Jesus Christ to die.*

Here is a miracle we see each day. The miracle that God loved us and sent his Son. The miracle that Jesus died for sinners. The miracle that his death continues to cleanse us from sin. Through him we perform a miracle, the miracle of discipleship. By his power we die each day. We take the cross. We feel its power and its wonder. Each day we gaze at the cross as this centurion did and we confess what he confessed: "Surely this was, surely this is, the Son of God."

The greatest miracle of all.

CHAPTER THIRTEEN

AN UNEXPECTED RETURN

Luke 24:13-35

"Were not our hearts burning within us . . . ?" Luke 24:32

"**E**xpect a miracle!"

So said a famous revivalist of our day. However, when one returns to biblical times, one finds that the disciples rarely expect a miracle. They had witnessed Jesus healing the lepers, stilling the storm, and raising the dead. Yet when he dies, they flee in fright, thinking all is over.

No one expected the resurrection.

Jesus clearly predicted his resurrection, but when it happened no one expected it. The women came to the tomb to anoint a dead body, not to greet a risen Lord. They worried over how they would roll away the stone; they didn't know it was already removed. Even after seeing the empty tomb and hearing the news of the resurrection from the young man in the white robe, they flee the tomb in fright, "trembling and bewildered" (Mark 16:8).

No one expected his appearances. The two on the road to Emmaus at first don't even recognize the risen Lord. The apostles are cowering in fear even *after* they hear of the resurrection. When he appears, it always startles, always catches them off guard. The Jesus who was a constant surprise during his life continues to shock after his death and resurrection.

We may marvel at the slowness of the disciples. If Jesus said he would rise again (and he did), why didn't they expect it? Why was it so hard to believe? How could they be so hardhearted and hardheaded?

We'd better not be too tough on these early disciples. We might find the stones we throw rebounding in our own direction. Jesus clearly predicted his death and resurrection. Just as clearly he predicted his return at the end of the age. They were caught off guard by the empty tomb and the risen Lord. We must not be caught off guard by the last trumpet and the returning Lord. As we look again at the startled faces of the disciples who saw their crucified Lord alive, let us resolve to live in expectation of the time when every eye will see him. That great miracle is still to come.

Heartburn

It was a strange and perilous journey.

It began with two friends, setting out for Jerusalem for the feast of Passover. They had made the journey together before; it had been neither strange nor perilous.

But this time it was different. This time things happened in Jerusalem that had never happened before. Strange things that would change their lives.

It began the day they arrived. Coming into the city they noticed a commotion. A crowd was rushing out the gate. "What's happening?" they wondered, and finally got the courage to ask a passing woman.

"It's Jesus from Nazareth," she breathlessly replied, "He's coming into the city, riding a donkey like a king."

"What do you mean, 'Like a king?'" But she had already rushed away.

Deciding to see for themselves, they pushed through the crowd to the roadside. Many had stripped the nearby palm trees for their branches.

And then he came.

He looked in many ways like any other man. And yet. And yet there was something about him, a presence, an authority. As he got closer, the crowd went wild, placing palm branches in his path and calling him the Son of David.

"Who is this Jesus?" they wondered.

In the days to come they were to find out. They watched open-mouthed as he overturned the money-changers' tables in the temple. They witnessed his contests of wits with the scribes and Pharisees. They even visited with his disciples and learned of his miracles, of his teaching, and of his kingdom. Finally they were convinced. In this, the strangest week of their lives, they had come to believe that this rabbi from Nazareth was the one they had sought. He was the Savior, the Messiah.

They were there when he was killed.

Having placed all there hopes on him, they saw their hopes die with him, locked away forever in a garden tomb.

But then came the strangest part of all. Some of the women disciples told them they had found the tomb empty and that angels had appeared and told them that Jesus was alive.

The two friends didn't believe them. Having made the perilous journey to faith only to have that faith crushed, they were not about to believe such a story. Jesus may have had the power to heal and even to raise others from the dead, but it was too much to believe that he was alive again. They had watched him die.

So they started home.

They walked in silence for a while, then began to discuss this week that had turned them inside out. They were overtaken by a stranger. He was going their way and asked if he could tag along. "Sure," they said.

"I couldn't help but notice you were deep in conversation when I interrupted you. What were you talking about?"

"Oh, about this past week in Jerusalem."

"What about it?"

"Oh, you know, about Jesus of Nazareth."

"What about him?"

"You've come from Jerusalem and don't know about Jesus?"

So they told the stranger of their incredible week, how they had pinned all their hopes on this Jesus, but it had all come to nothing. He had been killed.

"But wasn't the Messiah supposed to be killed?" he asked. And he began to give them the most marvelous Bible lesson they had ever heard, quoting Scriptures from Moses to the prophets.

Soon it was supper time and they invited the stranger to eat with them at a local inn. At first he said no, but they finally convinced him. At the meal, he took the bread, blessed it, broke it, and gave it to them.

And then it happened. Suddenly they saw him clearly. It was Jesus! Alive! Their hope was not in vain.

As soon as they recognized him, he disappeared. Leaving supper on the table, they hurried back to Jerusalem to tell his disciples.

"We should have known sooner," they said, "for while he talked with us on the road, our hearts burned within us."

A familiar story. But the story of these disciples is our story too. Like them we have come to faith in Jesus, some of us quickly, some slowly, some easily, some with difficulty. And like them we may have our doubts. We too wonder, "Is he truly the Messiah? Did he really rise from the dead? Can this miracle be believed?" It seems too good to be true. We want so much to believe it that we worry that it may be just wishful thinking.

How can we be sure Jesus is the Son of God? One can give many logical proofs, can make many good arguments, but how can we know?

We know because our hearts burn within us. By faith

we have seen Jesus, we have heard his voice along the roads of our own lives. We have recognized him at his table when the bread is broken. At times we may be blind. Like these two friends, we do not recognize him. But even in those times of doubt, our eyes are opened. Looking back, we too can only wonder how we failed to see him. For his words burn deep into our hearts.

Locked Doors

They'd just gotten the news.

Mary of Magdala had returned from the tomb and announced, "I have seen the Lord!" (John 20:18). Breathlessly she told them of her early morning visit. She had found the tomb empty and had run to Peter and John in distress. "Someone's taken the Lord's body and we don't know where it is!" Peter and John ran to the tomb and found it as she described. It was empty. They returned to their homes wondering what it meant.

But Mary had returned to the tomb, distraught. Crying bitterly, she wondered, "Why can't they just leave him alone? They've even taken his body before we can give it a proper anointing." She wept from sorrow and rage. She decided to look in the tomb one more time. Maybe she'd just imagined it. Maybe he was really there.

And there was someone there! Two someones dressed in white. "Why are you crying?" they asked.

"They have taken my Lord away and I don't know where they have put him."

Suddenly she noticed someone behind her. "Who are you looking for?" he asked.

"Finally," she thought, "here's someone who can help." She thought he was the caretaker. If anyone knew what had happened to Jesus' body, it was he. "If you put his body somewhere, just tell me where he is and I'll get him," she cried.

"Mary," he said.

And in that one word she recognized him.

In joy she held him until he had to tell her to let go. "Tell the others," he said.

So she did. She ran and told the disciples who were meeting in the upper room.

They met at night. In secret. Behind locked doors. Afraid of the Jewish authorities. After all, they'd seen what had happened to Jesus. None of them wanted to be crucified.

One would think that Mary's news would have changed all that. If Jesus is risen, then whom should they fear? Perhaps it was their lack of faith, perhaps cowardice, perhaps an understandable caution. For whatever reason, the doors were locked.

Suddenly Jesus stood among them. He was no ghost! They saw his wounded hands and side. They were beside themselves with joy. The Lord is alive! Jesus even breathes the Holy Spirit upon them. Then he disappears.

Now they had seen him themselves. Now the Spirit was upon them. Now we expect them to have faith and courage. But one was not there. Thomas refuses to believe unless he can put his own hands in the wounds of Jesus. So a week later they are in the house again.

The doors were locked.

Why? Had they learned nothing? Were they still afraid? It appears so. Thomas is the one called "doubting," but in spite of what they had seen and what had been given to them, the other disciples locked the door. What were they afraid of? If God can raise Jesus from the dead, what enemy can overcome them? What's the worst thing that could happen to them? Torture? Death? Jesus endured both and now stands before them a second time. Alive!

Being an eyewitness of the resurrection didn't keep them from fear. The Holy Spirit did not give them the confidence to leave the doors unlocked. We marvel at their lack of trust. Have we more faith than they?

Thomas sees and believes. Jesus says, "Because you have seen me, you have believed; blessed are those who have not seen and yet have believed" (John 20:29). Do you believe in the resurrection? Then Christ blesses you. Do you believe in the resurrection? Then why do you fear? Why lock your doors?

There's nothing sinful about locking the doors to our cars, our homes, our offices. It is prudent to do so. But how many of us claim to be Christians, believers in a risen Lord, and continue to live our lives in fear? We lock the doors of our hearts to anyone and anything that might threaten. We put our trust in safety and precautions, not in the God who raised Jesus from the dead.

What's the worst that can happen to us? We'll be hurt. Abused. Taken advantage of. Cheated. Robbed. Unjustly imprisoned. Beaten. Killed. Or perhaps the worst that will happen is we'll live our lives feeling unfulfilled, unappreciated, facing midlife crises and a slow end in a nursing home. God delivered Jesus from death. Can he not deliver us from whatever it is we fear? Won't he?

He will. He does. And we dare not live our lives like these fearful disciples. We believe in this great miracle of resurrection. He lives! He lives for us. We live now and will live again through him.

He stands at the door and knocks.

Unlock the door.

Let him in.

The Expected Jesus

Jesus was a man of miracles, signs, and wonders. The disciples saw the miracle of the resurrection and believed. We did not see, yet we believe. We believe because our hearts burn within us. We believe because, like Mary, we have heard him call our names. We have opened the door and let him into our hearts. By faith we see he still works wonders in our lives. There is still one great wonder to come.

The surprising Jesus is coming again. We don't know when. It will be a surprise, but it must not be one to us. He says, "Be ready."

How often do we even think about the coming of the Lord? How often do we talk of it? I confess I can go whole weeks without the thought crossing my mind. I hear few Christians speak of the Second Coming. I hear fewer sermons on the subject. Instead it appears that many of us live our lives as Christians as if this world will last forever.

What does it mean to be ready? Should we try to live each moment of each day with the conscious thought, "The Lord may come today?" I don't think we can. I don't even think we should. But the thought should be there behind our conscious thoughts, informing all that we do.

Many of us know what it's like to wait for a child to be born. The anticipation of our child's birth affects all we do or say or think months before his actual birth. As time grows closer, we go about our normal business, but always in the back of our minds is "This might be the day." It's the same with the Lord's coming. We know it's soon; we don't know when.

So he encourages us to be ready. We stay ready not by constantly asking, "Will it be today?" but by living lives of quiet obedience, so that whenever he comes, we will be found faithful. We stay ready by doing. We stay ready by remembering his teachings, his miracles, and his life. By reflecting on the real Jesus, the one who astounded his contemporaries, we begin to recognize him. We see him in the lives of those around us, we hear his voice in the words of Scripture, we feel his presence with us in prayer, we rely on his help when tempted. By following his steps we are being transformed in his image. By walking with him, we are being prepared for that day when we shall see him face to face.

That great miracle is coming.

We expect him.

May he come quickly!

CHAPTER FOURTEEN

A CHURCH OF SIGNS AND WONDERS

Acts 2:42-47

"*. . . many wonders and miraculous signs were done by the apostles*" *Acts 2:43.*

Miracles, signs, and wonders. We've followed Jesus as he heals the blind, casts out demons, multiplies food, and even raises the dead. Through faith we have seen his miracles. Wouldn't it be wonderful if we could go back in time and see them with our own eyes? We envy those early disciples who were eyewitnesses.

Some of those eyewitnesses did more than see God's miraculous power in Jesus. They experienced that power themselves. On Pentecost, the sound of a tornado fills the room, tongues of fire appear, the Holy Spirit fills some of the disciples and they speak in other tongues. On that day Peter tells the crowd of Jesus, one ". . . accredited by God to you by miracles, wonders, and signs" (Acts 2:22). Peter calls them to faith in Jesus. Three thousand respond and are baptized. The church begins with miracles.

We envy those eyewitnesses of Jesus. We envy the apostles who worked wonders and signs. We have no apostles around today. We may not see the blind healed or the dead raised with our own eyes.

Or do we? I have never seen one born blind receive his sight. I've never seen one raised from the dead. I have seen Jesus work in my life and in the lives of those around me. I've prayed for the sick. He healed them. I've begged for forgiveness. He cleansed me. I've asked for wisdom. He guided me. He works in amazing ways, miraculous ways. He still works wonders.

By faith we see the hand of Jesus still healing the sick. What's more, by faith we see the miracles of Jesus and the apostles in the New Testament. These are not simply miracles of long ago. They are stories of a risen, active Savior.

What difference do these miracles of long ago make in our lives today? What have we learned from these stories? Must we live differently now that they are a part of us?

To answer these questions, let's look at the difference the miracles made to the first church. The church in Jerusalem was built upon the one who did wonders, signs, and miracles. It was led by apostles who did the same. How did they respond to these miracles? Luke tells they responded by devoting themselves to certain things.

The proper response to miracle is devotion. We hear the word "devotion" often today. We speak of worship periods as "devotionals," talk of "devotional Bible studies," and may even call this book a "devotional book." What do we mean? If we don't take care, we may mean something different from the biblical use of the word. To many, "devotional" implies an outburst of enthusiasm. Unfortunately, such enthusiasm doesn't last long. Soon we need another "devotional" study to pump us up again spiritually.

Miracles caused excitement and enthusiasm. The early church transformed that momentary enthusiasm into permanent devotion. To be devoted to something means to make it a constant practice. It implies dedication, discipline, and habit. The Jerusalem Christians experienced the thrill of miracle, but they wanted more. From them we learn to devote ourselves to a life of discipleship. A life of more.

Learn More

"They devoted themselves to the apostles' teaching . . ." (Acts 2:42). These first believers had come to Jerusalem from all over the world to celebrate Pentecost. While there they found their lives radically changed. Now they believed that Jesus was the promised Messiah they had awaited.

But what did they know of Jesus? Some perhaps had seen his miracles and heard his teaching. Others knew very little. They might not have known that Jesus healed the lame, cast out demons, and raised the dead. They may not have heard that he taught, "Love your enemies." They had been baptized in his name. They had dedicated their whole lives to him. They wanted to know more of this Messiah who saved them.

Who's going to teach them? Who better than the apostles? They had been with Jesus. They had seen his signs and heard his teaching. They were witnesses to his resurrection. No wonder these early Christians wanted to sit at their feet and learn of the Savior. We can hear their questions to the apostles.

"What did Jesus do then?"

"How did he answer the Pharisees?"

"Did he really mean it when he said to turn the other cheek?"

"What was it like to see that young girl come back to life?"

By faith we see the miracles of Jesus. We hear his teaching. If we want to know more, we go to the same source as these first believers. We go to the teachings of the disciples about Jesus. We read those teachings in the Gospels, and the more we read and reflect and pray, the more we want to know about our Savior.

Are we devoted to the apostles' teaching? Do we want to know more of Jesus? Of course. By looking at his miracles, we are moved to dedicate ourselves to study so we may know him more.

Share More

These first believers were dedicated to fellowship. Many of us can't separate the word "fellowship" from eating. It conjures up memories of church suppers, potlucks, and dinners on the ground. These Pentecost believers also ate together from house to house. Three thousand converts at Pentecost. Many of them must have been strangers to each other. How do you get to know someone? By sharing a meal. By "doing lunch." We still do it that way today.

But fellowship is more than eating together. The Greek word here is one of the few that most Christians know, *koinonia*. It is best translated "sharing." These Christians shared their food, but they shared much more. They even shared their money. "Selling their possessions and goods, they gave to anyone as he had need" (Acts 2:45). Here is the true test of Christian fellowship: Are you willing to cash in your investments to help a Christian brother or sister? These early disciples, though strangers to each other, were willing even to share their goods.

Most importantly, they shared their faith. This is what they had in common: they all had come to faith in Jesus. So they shared their food, their possessions, their inmost thoughts, their very lives. What brought them together was not their similarities, what they had in common. What brought them together was the miraculous power of Jesus. Because they wanted to know him more, they also wanted to share with each other more.

Pray More

These converts at Pentecost were all Jews. They knew how to pray. They still needed to learn to pray as Jesus prayed. Many of them knew little of Jesus' teachings on prayer. Imagine hearing the Lord's Prayer for the first time. Imagine their surprise when they heard they must pray even for their enemies. These converts learned to pray from Jesus by way of the apostles. They learned to devote themselves to prayer.

The apostles were more than teachers of prayer. They practiced what they preached. A dispute arose in the church concerning the distribution of food to widows. The church appointed seven men to feed the widows so the apostles could "give [their] attention to prayer and the ministry of the word" (Acts 6:4). Fellowship, that is, sharing with the poor is certainly an act close to the heart of God. So is prayer. The early church neglected neither. Like Jesus before them they developed a habit of prayer.

What power these early Christians had! What fellowship! What was their secret? The miraculous power of Jesus? Of course. Their experience of the Spirit? Certainly. But they also knew the secret of prayer. The early church was a praying church. That was the source of their power. If we are to recapture their faith and their witness, we must learn to be devoted to prayer. We want to pray more to a powerful Father. We want to pray more with a loving Savior. We want to pray more in the power of the Spirit.

Worship More

The early church met to worship God in the name of the Lord Jesus. The wonders and miracles of Jesus and the apostles were signs. They pointed to the love and power of the heavenly Father. At the miraculous catch of fish, Peter faced that holy power and love in the person of Jesus. He responded in fear, falling at Jesus' feet and saying, "Go away from me, Lord; I am a sinful man!" (Luke 5:8). Thomas faced that holy power in the resurrected Jesus and worshipped, saying, "My Lord and my God!" (John 20:28).

These believers saw the power of God in the miracles of Pentecost. They react with fear. "Everyone was filled with awe . . ." (Acts 2:43). Holy fear is the ground of worship. "But why should we fear God?" you ask. "Isn't he a loving Father?" Yes. Oh, yes. But he is also the Almighty. He is an awesome God. "Awesome" has lost much of its original punch. Today we call everything from the latest fashions to the newest car "awesome." Perhaps some older translations are closer to the mark when they call God an "awful" God. He is not awful in the contemporary sense of the word, but he is one who inspires fear, awe, reverence.

When we see the power of God in the miracles of Jesus we are awestruck. They bring us to our knees in worship. We bow before a God whose holiness and power scare us.

How do we express that reverent fear? These early Christians expressed it in the breaking of the bread. As we saw above, this phrase refers to eating together with fellow Christians. It also refers to eating with Jesus. At the Lord's Supper we come in contact with the Holy One of Israel. To the early church, the Lord's Meal was so central to their worship, that their entire purpose for meeting is summed up in the phrase, ". . . we came together to break bread" (Acts 20:7).

Each Sunday we witness a miracle. Jesus comes and eats with us! We share a meal with the one who stilled the waves, multiplied the loaves, and even defeated death. How can we approach this meal except with awe? How can we leave without wanting to worship him more?

Rejoice More

The Jerusalem church had "glad and sincere hearts" (Acts 2:46). They were happy people, but they had more than their share of trouble. Christian happiness is not based on circumstances. It is a miracle. Christ alone makes our hearts glad. These early Christians would soon know persecution. Some, like the apostles, would be beaten and thrown in jail. Some, like Stephen, would even give their lives for the faith. No matter. They still were happy. After the apostles are flogged by the Sanhedrin, they leave "rejoicing because they had been counted worthy of suffering disgrace for the Name" (Acts 5:41).

How do we react when we see the miracles of Jesus? We rejoice. We dedicate ourselves to him even if it means suffering. If hard times come because of Jesus, our hearts are still glad. We suffer because he suffered for us. Here is happiness the world can never understand, not the shallow happiness that all experience when things are going great. No, this is the deep and powerful joy that comes when the wonderful power of Jesus lives in us. He died for us. We died with him. He was raised for us. We were raised with him. He gives us the miracle of new hearts. Hearts of gladness and joy.

Grow More

We hear much today about church growth. Every year it seems a new technique comes along as a sure-fire way to make new converts. All Christians want the church to grow because, like God himself, we want all people to be saved. We have seen the signs of Jesus in our lives, so we want others to experience his saving power.

Yet we struggle with the how. How do we take the gospel to our neighbors? How can we let them know the joy we feel? How can we reach those who know about Jesus, but don't really know him? Like the Pharisees, they see his miraculous works, but can't see who he is. How do we make the church grow?

The early Jerusalem church was a growing church. It begins with three thousand. Soon afterward their number grows to five thousand (Acts 4:4). Eventually they must have given up counting, for Luke simply says, "The number of disciples in Jerusalem increased rapidly . . ." (Acts 6:7).

How do we explain this rapid growth? Did these Christians evangelize? I'm sure they did. They overcame their fear to tell their neighbors the good news of Jesus.

Did they grow because of the wonders done by the apostles? No doubt those miracles convinced many. But what was their real secret of church growth?

Their secret was this: they were devoted to Jesus, not to growth. As Luke puts it: "And the Lord added to their number daily those who were being saved" (Acts 2:47).

The Lord added. It's not our church. It's the Lord's church. Church growth is not our job. It's his. He alone works the miracle of salvation in the hearts of human beings. Our part is to witness to what he has done for us. We tell others of his wonders. He works the wonder in them. His power is not limited by how well we tell the story or what techniques we use to motivate others to believe. Like the apostles, we are to tell the story of Jesus. The old, old story. We tell it clearly. We tell it boldly. But the power is in the story, not in our telling. The power, the sign, the wonder of Jesus and his love.

Complacency, Excitement, or Devotion?

When we look at the miracles, we have a choice. We can react with complacency. Even boredom. We've heard all this before. It is an old, old story to many of us. We can look at the miracles of Jesus and feel nothing.

Or we can see them through fresh eyes. Like the blind man, we can feel the touch of Jesus and see what we could not see before. We can catch some of the excitement the original witnesses felt as they saw these amazing acts. What is more, we feel the excitement of knowing Jesus still works in our lives today. We may not understand why or how, but we know he is there for us. In the words of H.W. Farrington:

> *I know not how that Bethlehem's Babe*
> *Could in the Godhead be;*
> *I only know the manger Child*
> *Has brought God's life to me.*

I know not how that Calvary's cross,
A world from sin could free;
I only know its matchless love
Has brought God's love to me.

I know not how that Joseph's tomb
Could solve death's mystery;
I only know a living Christ,
Our immortality.

That excitement might last for moments, perhaps even for days. It will not last forever. It must be turned into something permanent. In Jesus' day, there were those who witnessed the miracles, who were amazed, who were excited, but they never became disciples. The miracles are there to give us faith. Faith in the one who still works wonders. It must be a faith that wants more. A faith that is devoted, no matter what the cost. We want not the sign, but the one the sign points to. We want not a wonder, but one named Wonderful. We want the greatest miracle of all.

A miracle named Jesus.

ABOUT THE AUTHOR

Gary Holloway is Director of Graduate Bible Studies, Lipscomb University, Nashville, Tennessee. Formerly he served as Associate Professor at the Institute for Christian Studies in Austin, Texas and ministered with the Holland Street Church of Christ in San Marcos. Gary received the B.A. from Freed-Hardeman College, the M.A.R. from Harding Graduate School of Religion, the M.L.I.S. from the University of Texas, and the Ph.D. from Emory University.